What Others Are Saying About This Book

"This book is a must for every parent or future parent. It should be required reading for teachers and be given as a present to every adult."

Jason Brooks, University professor, Texas

"This book has paid for itself a hundred times over with what I have gained from it. I have begun to use some of the methods in my class and they work!"

Karen Fleming, teacher, Hawaii

"I would love to have my kids experience a class like that. On second thought; to heck with the kids—I want to be in that class!"

Dan Fitzgerald, Ph.D., Psychologist, New York

"I believe that each reader will pull a different concept out of the book—whatever one they need at that time in their life."

Cathy Chamberlain, Parent-student, Montana

"Tired of dry theories on why the educational system is failing our children? Dr. Starkey's humorous and entertaining account of his practical classroom success teaches you to get innovation in gear and jump aboard for an exhilarating—and fulfilling—ride."

Diana Tüchsen-Brown, Educator, California

"What they see is what you get. Kids learn by the models in their world—that is, by what they hear and see others do. The author clearly demonstrates the vast importance of this learning trait in children."

James Wilson, Education Consultant, Tennessee

"Wonderful! Every story in this book is worth a thousand pictures."

Gabriel West, poet/artist, Connecticut

". . . funny, original, and enlightening—an honest contribution to the teaching profession."

Donna Taylor, Marketing Consultant, Texas

Will The Real Teacher Please Stand Up?

Teaching Stories For More Effective Education

By R. Hawk Starkey, Ph.D.

First Edition

The author and Inreach Publishing hold no liability or responsibility to anyone in respect to any loss or damage caused or alleged to be caused directly or indirectly by any information or concepts contained in this book.

Published by

Inreach Publishing
P.O. Box 33280, #288
Austin, Texas 78764

Illustrated by Robert Lopez
Typesetting and layout by MacPages Austin, Texas
Printed in the USA by McNaughton & Gunn, Inc.

Library of Congress Catalog Card Number: 93-80684
ISBN: 0-9639447-4-6

This book is dedicated to Parents:

First of all to my own parents, who have always honored and enriched me with the freedom to be who and what I must be, while unconditionally accepting me for such.

Secondly, this book is dedicated to the parents of all my past students. For their backing and willingness to help and to accept my "off-the-wall" experimental programs in the classroom, and for providing the gremlins without which this book could never have existed.

And last but not least, to all parents everywhere. May you be blessed with the ability to persevere, the insight to recognize your children and yourself as loving, caring, deserving human beings, and may you have the wisdom to see the child as the real teacher.

TABLE OF CONTENTS

	Acknowledgments	11
	Preface	12
	Introduction	13
1	The Day I Sold The Classroom	15
2	Ahab The Arab And Bach	19
3	Teachings	22
4	Draw Your Thumb	25
5	Write-In Books	30
6	Little Desks All In A Row	35
7	How To Throw A Fit	39
8	Poet And Don't Know It	41
9	AAAs . . . And Secretaries	45
10	More On Secretaries	49
11	Tell Me, How Do You Tie A Shoelace?	52
12	With Your Permission, May I Tell You A Lie?	54
13	No Homework, If . . .	58
14	The View From The Top Of The Desk	60
15	Free Time—You Can Buy It!	62
16	The Project Box	67
17	Turkey Feast	70

18	The Value Of Solitude	72
19	Community Work Experience Program	76
20	Squares Of The Wall For Sale	80
21	My Box	83
22	Lamps Are So Simple	86
23	We Had A Bank—Sure	88
24	We Also Had A Class Store	93
25	A Real Creep	97
26	The Day We Had A Hanging	99
27	Never Picked Last	102
28	Hoax	104
29	This Newspaper Reporter Came To Interview Me	108
30	Mechanics Workshop	112
31	I Feared For My Car In The Parking Lot	115
32	A Hard Act To Follow	120
33	A Very Special Privilege	125
34	Think Tank	128
35	The End Of School	131
	Epilogue	134
	Notice	140
	Index	141
	About The Author	143

Acknowledgments

I would like to thank my parents for the role models they provided me throughout my growing up. My many years of observing from backstage while they performed on stage, in vaudeville and early television helped prepare me for the time I would be on and performing as a teacher/learner in the classroom. I couldn't have been given a greater advantage.

Special thanks and appreciation go to my chief editor, business partner and closest friend, Laura. She has lived with every step and stage of the process; respecting my needed times of silent writing, magically producing delicious and nutritious meals, offering constructive criticism, and so effectively managing the business. I'm sure glad she's my wife—I could never afford to pay her otherwise.

Thanks to my own children. They have taught me more than they'll ever know. I love them dearly.

My appreciation to Inreach Publishing for their hard work and quality job of publishing.

Sincere thanks to my publishing consultant, Daena Poppitt, owner of MacPages in Austin, Texas, for her unshakable faith in this book and in her ability to pull it all together in the best way possible.

To Amy Phillips, typesetter and assistant editor, I extend much appreciation and thanks; for she had a most challenging task of deciphering my left-handed scribblings.

Thanks to Robert Lopez, illustrator and artist who was able to take my vision and capture it on an art pad for all to see and share.

To David, my deepest gratitude: principal and human being extraordinaire.

Thanks to Dr. Patrick O'Bryon, Dani O'Bryon, Dr. Bill Hamilton, Dr. Robert Leos, Donna Taylor, and to the many others not mentioned here, for their valuable contributions of thought, suggestions and corrections.

Preface

Teaching, in any form, is a business to be taken with utmost seriousness of intent, and with a clear view of the cause and effect of what one does.

Do not be misled by what may appear as simple, easy or "off the cuff" in this book. Much time, study, trial and error were invested by the author in order to develop an effective and successful personal style of communicating with students, including children who can be incorrigible or challenging to work with. And each student is different. The need to be constantly aware of the impact and effect of one's every word, expression and action at all times cannot be stressed enough. Such must become habit and as second nature when interacting with young minds.

Professional integrity, self-examination (on a daily basis), self-knowledge, self-honesty and personal growth are all of the utmost importance. You have only to work on yourself. If you want to be a better teacher/parent become a better person. And remember, it's all one step at a time. We don't make "mistakes," we only have experiences. Allow yourself one minute of discouragement at a time. Time yourself for that minute, end it, and get on with your growth.

Unless you are ready to dedicate not just your life but your very being to development, continued self-education, constant questioning, and reevaluation of all things, along with the unending search for truth, meaning and quality, you should seriously reconsider any thought about being a teacher, parent or adult.

Is it too late to reconsider? No problem—you are already embarking upon the journey to excellence by reading this book.

Congratulations, your foot is on the path. Good luck.

Introduction

Welcome to our fourth-, fifth-, and sometimes sixth-grade combination, self-contained class. I'm your tour guide for today and I will be happy to show you around. We are pleased to have you visit with us and we invite you to be a part of our class while you are here . . .

Come, step through the looking glass and enter with me into a special world of high-rise seating with desk lamps, cushioned trash cans, Beethoven, Bach, and Ahab the Arab. Come in and browse around. Would you like to see the insides of a carburetor, or maybe disassemble a typewriter?

Did you know that four of us once formed a corporation and actually purchased the classroom? Or that we sometimes have a creep in the class? Also, you can pay someone to throw a fit for you, if you are so inclined.

. . . And, if you see a large white rabbit with a big watch, just ignore him—he's really not there at all.

Chapter One
The Day I Sold The Classroom

It was a rather impromptu thing on my part and I could only play it by ear as I watched it unfold. It all started during one of our regular class discussions, a discussion that would somehow begin and develop into an interesting and rewarding encounter on a regular, but unplanned, basis. I have forgotten what this particular session was about, but somewhere it was mentioned that since I was the teacher I was also boss of the class. Expanding upon that concept, I asked if, as "boss," did I also "own" the class, say, as a landlord might be in charge of office space?

It was agreed that, yes, I was like a landlord and I asked, "Could I charge 'rent' for use of desks and certain areas of the classroom?" The response was an immediate and energetic, "Yes! I'll pay you to be on the second level of the 'dock'" (a split level wood structure that seated four on top and four below, carpeted, posts and all, with remnants donated by parents). "I'll pay rent to sit under the high-rise," came another bid. The "high-rise" was another two-story structure the kids and I had built from parent-donated materials, which not only had a ladder built in for upper level access, but also a climbing rope as an alternative. Offers to rent or lease were coming at me from every section of our unique classroom.

The kids had the funds to back up their offers. Some of them were quite wealthy indeed, but what use did I have for their "money"? We had a very complete and intricate monetary system in the class. Kids earned a money called "marks" (a little pun on the German mark, and its lack of value at one time in wartime Germany). Marks were credits on the books for projects and class work. The kids received letter grades on assignments and I felt that grades were worth marks as well. We had a student-run banking system; checking, savings, interest, receipts and all, as well as a class store in which to spend the marks. I'll get into all that in greater depth, later on.

As it turned out, I decided that I was tired of being "landlord" and dealing with the headache of distributing and rotating seats in a fair and just manner. While all seating areas were cozy, with carpet, lamps, couches, and lounges, some were special and in constant demand. So I offered to sell the classroom seating areas. Whereupon four of the wealthiest students formed a corporation and out-bid all others.

The four new landlord tycoons, two boys and two girls, had mark signs in their eyes as they held an executive board meeting (us four and no more) to decide what rent they should charge for seating. Needless to say, their ambition and profit expectations were high. So was their request for rent. A few of the more wealthy students were willing to pay, at first inclination, but soon joined the rest of the class in a rent boycott when they realized that their earnings would all go to supporting the landlords. There would be no more marks to buy quality goods from the store, or for

purchasing extra free time for play or use of the "Mechanics Fix-It Shop" (another story).

With just the appropriate amount of huff, to show their indignation toward the new landlords, all the students removed their books and belongings from their desks and found a spot outside the "owned property" areas. Some settled in the reading area, others on the couch or under the library table, some in the "fix-it" workshop (the high-rise concept gave us extra room for such things), and others on various places of the carpeted floor. Two girls settled down in the two Pontiac bucket seats mounted on top of a large carpeted storage box, while one boy delightedly snuggled into a large rubber 50-gallon "trash" container half-filled with large pillows.

Our four new business entrepreneurs sat in their new property with just the right amount of smugness upon their faces (did I detect a moment of concern from time to time?), as they enjoyed their wealth and position, playing it for all it was worth.

The day continued with business as usual, and everybody seemed to be quite content with the new arrangement. Did I detect fading mark signs in four pairs of eyes?

Then, during a period of quiet study, the principal happened to pop in. He didn't even get completely through the door before he froze in his tracks. The class was quite used to regular visits from parent tutors, newspaper reporters, and from those who read what the newspaper reporters wrote. The two members of the greeting committee looked up, saw that it was only the principal, who did not need a tour of the classroom, and went back to their studies. All wore a look of satisfied smugness and determination for a boycott against unfair rent—through to the end of the semester and the financial ruin of the landlords, if need be.

The principal, as fine and noble a person as ever there was, was always cautious when entering our classroom. He had a unique sense of not intruding upon situations where he was not sure what was going on, lest his presence disrupt the harmony of the moment. He quickly realized that he did not know what was going on. Looking towards me (maybe to see if I knew what was happening), he shrugged his shoulders and lifted his eyebrows. I returned the gesture, implying I also didn't know what was going on, and he quietly closed the door and retreated to the security of his office. He felt assured that it wasn't a mutiny. I could tell, because he walked and didn't run back to his office.

The boycott was resolved by the end of the day. The landlords gave in and negotiations were held as to what was fair rent. I was pretty much ignored through the whole procedure after the class realized, through my shrugging, that I wasn't going to solve anything for them. I wasn't a property owner any longer, except for my own desk and area (hadn't thought about selling that). All I was concerned about was that the negotiations be conducted in an orderly and caring fashion, with consideration and respect shown for all parties. But everybody already knew all that. I just leaned back and enjoyed.

Later that day, I happened to see the principal as I was passing through the teachers' room. He said, "Hi, how are you doing?" No question about the class—he was simply happy that it wasn't a mutiny and that I was safe and smiling.

I said, "Oh, just before you came by I had sold the classroom and the new owners were being boycotted. Their rent prices were too high."

He said, "Oh, yes, of course. Fair's fair." I never did explain it to him. The mystery was half the fun of it.

Chapter 2

Ahab The Arab And Bach

A stereo was donated to our class by a parent (ask and you shall receive) who had an extra one sitting around the house. Nothing fancy: walnut cabinet, turntable and radio, lots of speakers built in on both sides of the cabinet. Magnavox, I believe it was.

Often we would study and work to various classical masterpieces presented in FM stereo by the local public radio station. (Who says kids don't appreciate "good" music?) But by far, the most work was done to the tune of "Ahab the Arab," an old album brought in by one of the kids that was popular in the '70s.

Few will dispute the inspirational effect of music. The right music for the right activity can be a real motivator of mood and inspiration. In this case, Ahab and his camel Clyde, and a number of other humorous songs by the same artist, served as excellent inspiration to students and teacher alike.

On one occasion a very important lesson was learned. One of the students said to me, "Whenever I hear that music, I just want to get a good book and curl up on the sofa and read." It had been a habit of mine to put some relaxing background music on during quiet reading time, hoping to provide a "filter" to outside distractions and a peaceful setting for reading. It was then that I realized that the music was serving as a reminder of the quiet and peaceful joy of reading.

To myself, I thanked the student for my lesson, as I had a habit of doing. So often the line between student and teacher was blurred. I tried to keep it that way.

There were times when our reading hour would run over the regular period. Being a self-contained class (the only one, other than the primary grades, in the whole school), we had the freedom to adjust the time periods to suit the needs and moods of the class. Time could be adjusted to shorten or lengthen any period of the day. I could not justify turning off a need, a desire, an interest, like a flick of a switch. After all, what had I been working to stimulate in these kids if not interest in learning?

So time would be stretched to an extra half hour, sometimes an extra hour. Once, upon hearing that my class had spent over two hours engaged in quiet reading, another teacher commented to me, "Your class read for two hours? How did you get them to sit still for so long?"

On a number of occasions, time would not only be stretched but actually warped—like two full days of reading. This reading time warp began one morning by evolving into a magical zone best described as a "warp" in the fabric of time itself. The kids just didn't stop reading, so I let them read. This was not an avoidance factor to get out of other work—if it was, I would instantly recognize such avoidance as a danger signal for me. If, at any time, kids tried to get out of a task or particular subject, that challenged me to make it interesting enough so that they would want to do it, even beg to be "allowed" to do it!

I had learned to recognize and take advantage of the magical, time warp situations. Time dissolved and the recess bell rang, through one of Bach's pieces, two hours early, or so it seemed. Not much happened in the classroom. A couple of students quietly came over to the couch behind my desk, where I was sitting with three other students reading, and asked, in a whisper, if they could go out to

recess. I nodded as I looked around the classroom, catching the raised eyebrows of two other students, nodded once again, and they also quietly left the room. Three of them returned before the bell ending recess.

The time warp continued and the class rotated in a dance of unplanned order and choreography. Reading places changed from the couch or bean bag chair in the reading lounge, to one of the two bucket car seats, to the trash can with pillows inside it, to pillows on the carpeted floor, to a spot on the couch next to me, all with ease, grace and respect towards others, and with respect for self, in an unconscious display of self-responsibility.

From time to time, a quiet question or questioning look from a student and a nod from me allowed a trip to the restroom or playground (in full view of the classroom) for a jog or a stretch. Amid some protest, lunch time was accepted as a necessary break, although many took their books to find a grassy spot under a tree. Sensing their need and respecting the mostly non-verbal request of the class, I returned early. As a rule during such times, the entire class usually drifted quietly in before the bell.

The latter part of the day found more trips to the library by individuals, as one book was finished and another sought. No passes or notes of permission were needed. The reputation of the class was such that extra privileges were granted to the students by all, as the semester progressed and each student's reputation for self-responsibility evolved.

The second day passed as quickly as the first. More books were checked out of the library and many went home at night. Part way through the third day the warp ended—almost as though a switch had been thrown—"click." We looked at one another and suddenly the baseball diamond was the most attractive thing in the world. "Anybody for softball?" I asked. "Yeah," they said, and I stepped aside from the door and the rush to the field where we played with a renewed vigor (no, not for two days). As always, we rooted for the other team and cheered any strikeouts, missed catches, and flub-ups with loving fun for all.

Chapter 3
Teachings

Very early in the beginning of each school year, I would anxiously await the moment when a student asked me a question to which I didn't know the answer. I would say (almost proudly), "I don't know." The child would usually respond with, "But you're the teacher . . . ," assuming that teachers know everything.

I would say that I would like to find out, and that if he were to learn the answer, would he tell me (the challenge). The child would usually wander back to his or her desk, somewhat bewildered, but with the thought that it just might be possible to teach the teacher something.

Usually the rest of the class and I would have the answer by the following morning (the challenge answered). My response would be, "Thanks! That is really interesting to learn. Where did you find the answer?" (checking the research and validity), and the process began.

To reinforce the idea that kids can be self-learners and can actually teach others something of value (this includes parents and teachers), I devised something that I called "teachings." The idea originally came from a book that I read, written by Dr. Leo Buscaglia, noted author, psychologist, and promoter of humanistic and loving behavior among people. In his book he commented that his father asked him to teach him something every evening at the dinner table just before eating. Whether he had to "teach" for his supper or not, I don't know, but Leo felt that this practice was most beneficial for him as a child.

So, each morning began with my asking, "What can you teach me?" Each student was invited to have a tidbit of information that they hoped I may not have knowledge of. It was scary at first, for them as well as for me. If they really tried, they could make a real dummy out of me. But they were under the impression that I knew everything there was to know.

This was it. The contest between the students and the (dum da dum dum) TEACHER! The kids were nervous, giving each other looks of uncertainty and words of fearful encouragement. The teacher was calm, smug and self-certain—a college graduate.

The first question: "Did you know that frogs hibernate in the winter by burying themselves in the mud?"

Answer: "Yes."

The second question: (gulp) "Did you know that the moon has no air on it?"

Answer: "Yes."

Thoughts from the class: "We don't stand a chance."

Third question: "Did you know that the first bird (with feathers) was Archaeopteryx and that it lived about 150 million years ago?"

Answer: (gulp) "No."

"You didn't know that? Really?" the speaker of the question said in surprise. "No," I said, "thanks for teaching me. Where did you get your information?" (Always question.)

"From the World Book Encyclopedia, Volume A of 'Childcraft', page . . ."

Knew I should have gotten rid of those books. That kid was to become an expert on dinosaurs by the end of the semester. And he was going to teach me (and the class) everything he knew about them.

The tempo picked up from there and a general feeling of "can do" began to grow among the kids. I did my best to hold my own, but I must say the score was touch and go. They delighted in finding unique bits of information by some of the darndest research methods. One kid's dad was an M.D.—a surgeon or bone doctor of some sort. This kid was as bad as the dinosaur expert.

Periodically, he would insist on teaching me (while the class listened) a course on basic med. and boneology!—all to the delight of the class.

"Teachings" was one of many highly successful and effective programs used during my classroom teaching career. My criteria for judging the success of a program? The kids ate it up—they enjoyed it, learned and taught as a result of it, and interacted with interest and in a self-responsible manner with it. They were the ones to assess it.

Chapter 4

Draw Your Thumb

"There is one in every class," according to some old proverb. In my class there were usually two or three and sometimes a good half dozen. But then, I guess I asked for it—and hoped for it. What I'm talking about is the type of kid that delights in doing you one better. "Draw my thumb? Okay, I'll draw my thumb, heh, heh, heh."

I could almost read this kid's thoughts as he reached into his desk and brought out a large and powerful magnifying glass and began to study his thumb. He had just read the art assignment for the week and was planning how to get me—in the most humorous way possible.

"Draw your thumb!?" came the voice from the depth of the classroom. The hollow sound of the voice was due to its owner projecting it from the 50-gallon trash barrel as he lounged upon the royalty of numerous pillows. "My thumb? I have to draw my thumb for art?" he said.

The students were reading over the set of stapled sheets they were just handed, containing the week's assignments. This was a list and explanation of projects that they were each responsible for having done by the end of the week. There would be a history assignment from a chapter in their text, some science reading, a page of math, spelling, and the ever-challenging art assignment, just to name a few.

Groans and giggles were being expressed as the art project was turned to and read. It said: "Draw your thumb. Make a realistic sketch of your thumb."

"At least it's not as bad as last week," said one girl, "when we had to draw the bottom of our desk—without turning it over!"

Before that, the challenge was to draw the steel I-beam that ran across the ceiling of the classroom, the swinging seat, the faucet in the sink (only one existed in the room, so that took some group organizing on their part).

I sometimes used to sit at my desk, or on the couch behind it, and dream up great art projects. A few times I would get caught at it: "I can see it in your eyes. You're trying to think of an art project for us, aren't you?" I heard one time from a student. "We'll probably have to draw our big toe!" "Why thank you," I said, "that's a good one." More groans and a few requests for that particular student to not say anything else.

"Stop! You're giving him more ideas," a voice said. "Last month you gave him the brilliant idea of drawing an ant. That had us all lying on our bellies around an ant hole with our drawing pads."

One of the conditions on that project was that there was to be no interference of any kind with the ant. That included blocking the sun, due to my being taught by a student that ants navigated by the sun. I never did check that particular bit of info out for just how factual it was, but it was reason enough to give concern about how one life form may affect another; especially when one was a giant. (But then giants can be affected by five hundred thousand ants in one's home or on one's leg.)

This art project developed into a science project of each child picking an ant and following it on its

ventures for a period of time. This they were to record on paper, while not interfering or losing track of the ant. It was great fun for all. Even the ants enjoyed it, for they would do all kinds of interesting things such as collect food, move a carcass of a dead grasshopper they found, and even plan a raid on another ant colony and steal their larvae, all for our pleasure and benefit, I'm sure. This ant project led to a need for a science unit and in-depth study on ants.

How did I know there was a need to have a study on ants? The class demanded it, that's all.

"We just finished a unit on spiders, can't we do ants next?"

"Yeah, we know just about all there is to know about spiders—they're neat!"

"Why do ants do . . ." The questions started coming at me.

"I don't know," I said, "I haven't put a science unit together on ants as I did spiders. I thought we would just do insects in general next, I have that all ready to go."

"We'll do it! We'll research it out!" came a voice. Another chimed in, "Yeah, we can find everything there is to know about ants."

So a research committee was formed to learn and present a science unit about ants. It was a most thorough job, indeed, and most enlightening—not so much the ant unit as the team's ability to work effectively and affectionately, together.

The most difficult art project was, by far, the drawing of another person's tongue. It was difficult because it was so funny and so hard to hold one's tongue still. Would it be possible to draw the inside of another person's mouth? Hmm, might be the beginnings of a dental care science study.

Remember the kid with the magnifying glass? His poster of a larger-than-life, much larger-than-life, and much more life-like, thumb was to hang on the wall of the classroom for the rest of the semester.

The drawing had the quality of a cross between something Van Gogh might have done together with Escher. But it wasn't until one looked into the magnified crevasses and fissures of the well-used and unmanicured thumb, that one appreciated the mad artist. That is, an artist qualified to draw for Mad comics! There one would see small mountain (thumb) climbers roped together and scaling their way to the nail summit, pickaxes in hand. I believe the title was, "On Top of Ole' Digit." I was the third from the leader, and the one with the big thumbs. All thumbs, if one looked closely.

1. Kids do things for one main (and important) reason. Fun.

2. Kids find fun in things and people that are interesting, challenging, amazing, funny and "outrageous"—just to mention a few.

3. Kids learn faster, better and stay healthier when what they do is fun.

4. Show me a kid having fun and I'll show you a happy kid.

Now, change all the words beginning with "k" to the word "adults." Wasn't that fun?

Chapter 5
Write-In Books

The school storeroom at the top of the hill was one of my favorite haunts. It would, on a regular basis, produce great discarded goodies and unwanted treasures that other, more "normal" teachers could not use. Many hidden cast-offs lay in corners or between boxes covered with dust, neat things of unusual design and questionable usage, seldom seen by human eyes. But with a slight twist of the mind, a turn of the brain, they could be transformed into tools of education by an imagination run wild!

On one of my scavenging ventures, after letting myself in the (haunted?) storeroom on the hill with a secret key that came my way from a fellow teacher and fellow scavenger, I happened to come upon a most valuable treasure.

When the old crone gave me the secret key, she told me, in her raspy voice, that she had made regular raids on the storeroom for a number of years. "I've gotten all the good stuff," she said, "but knowing you (your strange mind), you may find something I've overlooked." As it was, she had overlooked a very special treasure indeed.

The key slid easily into the lock, turned with some difficulty and the door squeaked as I slowly pushed it open. It was dark and musty smelling inside. Spider webs were everywhere. My mind began to transform itself, to change in the most strange way. When I put that key in the lock I felt the change as I turned from teacher ("Dr. Jekyll") to scavenger ("Mr. Hyde").

In the back of that old room, in a dark and dusty corner, was an old bookcase covered with spider webs and dust. It was then that I saw a gnarled, bony hand slowly reaching up towards the top shelf of the bookcase. I held my breath as one bony finger, with a long crooked fingernail, reached out and hooked the top of one of the old dusty books on that shelf. My heart thumping fast, my breath rasping in my lungs, I tried to keep quiet lest somebody, or something, should notice my presence.

I suddenly thought of the old woman who gave me the key, and I wondered, what if she's in here? The hand was now removing the old dusty book from the top shelf and it was coming toward me, holding the book. I held my breath and reached out with my other bony hand, with the gnarled knuckles and long crooked fingernails, and with an explosion of breath I blew the dust from the cover of the book.

All of a sudden a scream sounded throughout the room, echoing off the dusty shelves and bouncing off the spider webs, making them vibrate back and forth, up and down. The laughing shriek sounded again as I tossed back my head and laughed a wild rasping cackle through my dry, dusty lips. "I found it!" came my dusty and cracking voice, "I found it, ha ha ha ha . . ."

Sitting down in an old dusty office chair with only two casters on the bottom of its legs, I tried to puzzle out what it was that I had found. I held the old book in a lone beam of dusty light that came in through a small grimy window. It was an outdated science book. The whole upper shelf was full of these books, and there were old outdated readers on the shelf below.

What to do with out-of-date textbooks? "Think," I said to myself, "think with the mind of Mr. Hyde." And that brain went to work. Opening the book, an old voice from my past said, "Do not write in books." That voice was the voice of an old teacher from my school days. As I removed a pencil from my pocket I thought to myself, "These books are waiting for the trash can. Last year a whole bookcase of books like these was thrown in the dumpster."

I began to read:

Alpaca

The alpaca is about ~~4~~ 14 feet tall.

(I changed 4 feet to "14" feet with my pencil. I like tall Alpacas.)

It looks like a tiny ~~person~~ kid in a

(I continued to cross out and change words)

big shaggy coat. In the ~~mountains~~ schools

of South America, where alpacas

live, ~~people~~ kids make ~~clothes~~ taffy of alpaca

wool. Alpacas are tame and are kept

in ~~herds~~ desks.

Suddenly, there was a loud ringing sound in my ears! The old scavenger is in here and she just hit me over the head with her broom because she has caught me with some of her treasures! No, that wasn't it at all. The bell to begin school just rang. With treasured science book in hand I left my "lab" and went to my classroom, once again as (Jekyll) teacher.

Handing the book to a student, I unlocked the classroom door, entered, and began to occupy myself with rearranging my desk and my thoughts for the day. In the corner of the reading area a child began to laugh. Others joined him as they read what was written (and edited by Hyde) in that old text.

One girl attempted to read it to others but could only sputter and gasp with laughter as tears ran from her eyes. That display caused others to begin to laugh as they passed the book around for all to read. Other attempts to read aloud were stifled by sputtering laughter as the imagery of the short story came alive in the mind's eye of the reader.

The boy to whom I originally handed the book wasted no time in claiming the book once again, and with pencil in hand began to alter the next story. One book was not going to be enough.

And so began "Write-in" books. The basic rules I printed in felt pen on the inside of the cover: "This is a Write-in book. Please use pencil only. You may change the words in a story, the title and even the author's name to your own. Please keep it neat, in good taste, and take care that your changes make sense."

Write-in books quickly became the rage and held their popularity throughout the year. Many a time we would howl with laughter as we sat in groups in one of our classroom lounges or reading areas, rewriting a story. We would begin sitting on the couch and literally end up on the floor, croaking with tears of laughter at our literature in the process of creation.

I have seen children recite poetry before the class from a Write-in book, with enough elegance and enunciation to win a contest. That was the easy part. The real challenge was to read it with a straight face. As often as not, the poem would be read with such mirth and sputtering that few words were clear enough to understand what was being laughed at. But that was okay. The mere sight of the orator holding a Write-in book was enough to begin a process of laughter within an audience in glorious expectation.

That very day I returned to the storeroom up on the hill. My secret key let me into its dark and dusty interior. Always aware of the possible presence of another seeker of treasures, I loaded my arms up with more (heh, heh, heh) Write-in books. My mind was filled with the value of the dusty treasures I held to my chest as I ambled back to the classroom, barely noticing the principal. He stood aside to let me pass as I chuckled to myself and sputtered dust from my nostrils.

"Heh, heh, heh, Write-in books!" I announced as I shuffled past him with dust covered hair all astray and eyes wild with discovery. "Write-in books," I shouted with the snaggle-toothed grin showing Hyde's stained and crooked teeth. (I better get it together before I get back to class, I thought to myself.)

The principal smiled nervously and nodded, assuring me that it was alright, "Yes, yes . . . of course. Glad to see everything is fine," he said—giving me plenty of room to pass by with my dusty hoard. ". . . Yes, of course . . ." as he scratched his head, suddenly remembering some important task awaiting him in his office. This time he ran.

Humans tend to settle into a routine, whenever given a chance, and act like machines. This may be comfort in the familiar or fear of the unknown—it doesn't matter, both will stifle growth. So you have to keep disturbing them. Besides, it is rather fun to gently rattle the cage once in a while. It keeps us on our toes.

Chapter 6
Little Desks All In A Row

I remember my first day as a credentialed teacher. After years of study and working in other teachers' classrooms while I was going to college, I at last stood in my own classroom. I had it all to myself, my own boss, a real teacher finally. Now, what do I do? The room was sterile and void; little desks all in rows awaiting little human bodies to sit in them, feet flat on the floor, hands folded, backs straight, and mouths shut only to open when spoken to . . . also with brains turned off, minds wandering and daydreaming, bottoms sore from the hard seat and wishing to be anywhere but here in school; hours to go . . . Let me out!

I opened my eyes and shook my head to clear out those memories of my internment in elementary school. This isn't going to do at all, I thought to myself. Something has got to be done; it's all too dull. We need some carpet—at least in one corner—some pillows to lounge upon and read . . . And so the reading corner developed with a mattress folded to form a futon style couch with a cover over it, carpet pieces, and various large pillows that came from parents when they heard of our needs.

The popularity of the corner grew from a reading area to a highly desired study area. I couldn't argue with the fact that this area was aesthetically more pleasing to be in than the bare floor and stark desks of the remainder of the room. I also could not dispute the fact that more and better quality work seemed to be happening in this area. Beyond a doubt, the kids were more peaceful, relaxed and at ease, and as a result, happier in such a home-like atmosphere.

The effect that this special area, with its newly added end tables, lamps and upholstered couch and chair, was having on all of us dawned upon me as I sat there correcting papers during an at-your-desk open book exam. From time to time a child would come to me for clarification of a problem or advice on an answer. Snuggling down on the couch beside me, he or she would ask the question, often holding my arm with cheek against my shoulder and all but begin to purr. We would talk about the question, and with a word of encouragement from me or a hug, a kind of calmness and peace began to prevail throughout the class. It said, this is a safe and protected place to be. There are no dragons here, you can relax your guard and just be yourself.

Our class members (myself included) had been, subconsciously, striving for beauty in our classroom environment. The problem facing us now was that we had out-grown our reading corner and study area. We needed more space like this favorite corner we had designed and were in the process of overusing. But then, I thought, shouldn't the entire classroom be a study area? A workshop and study area to suit our own special needs?

I put the thought to the class and the uproar of approval was rafter-shaking. I expected that such would be the case, and stressed the fact that we were not designing a playroom, but a more pleasant and comfortable environment in which to study, share, and learn. And, I thought to myself, a home-like atmosphere for all to encounter, respect and be proud of, especially those kids who may be lacking such in their private lives.

The class was soon transformed to an impressive degree, becoming a pleasant and productive environment, thanks once again to the help of parents with their generous donations of carpet, furniture and such. But it was the next year that we outdid ourselves.

The second year found the classroom undergoing a major change with the construction of such places as the high-rise seating areas, lounge/work areas, and mechanics fix-it workshop. The kids were excited by what was done the year before, and so were the parents. The word was out; more effective education was happening here. Wild and outrageous ideas were not so wild and off-the-wall, but effective in exciting kids to learn. Parents, the community, and the school board were behind me now. The principal was behind me from the beginning. His loving, trusting nature never faltered once during the time I knew him. With confidence and backing like that, I felt free to be more open about what we were doing in class.

Had I not received all this approval and support, would I have been so innovative in my teaching style? The answer is yes; to an extent, simply because I am innovative by nature. My methods wouldn't have been as effective and I may have been fired or quit, but yes, I would have, however with "closed doors," as many of the system's creative teachers do.

The janitor especially liked our room. He didn't have to clean it. With 35 or more janitor replicas it never took more than 5 minutes at the end of each day to do our housekeeping. No parent could ever dispute the value of the lesson in that exercise. We were proud of our "home" at school.

Small big,
Big small,
Your size doesn't matter at all, at all.
Wherever you go,
Whoever you meet,
Your size depends on the company you keep.

So went the poem from a Walt Disney animated movie; I remembered it from childhood.

This poem was to bring a smile and a ray of inspiration to a young boy in our class one day. He was small on the outside, for his age, but big on the inside. He just grew and grew and grew, for you see, he was in good company—lots of it.

Chapter 7

How To Throw A Fit

Matt was a little guy with a sense of humor and a sharp wit, but best of all he could throw a great fit! Matt had developed fit-throwing into a fine art, into a socially acceptable way of releasing tension, and into a great way of getting recognition and a good laugh. He was likable to the core, and will always be remembered by his fits on the floor.

Matt would constantly be put "out" in handball, four square and other games on the playground by larger and stronger kids. Frustrating indeed. To release his frustration he would lie down on the ground and for about three seconds kick his feet and pound his fists (carefully) and scream. Whereupon he would rise, brush himself off, walk to the end of the line, and calmly await his turn at the game once again, with the comment, "I feel much better now."

Quite often, other kids, in their attempt to get Matt "out" so they could see a real classic example of a fit, would instead get themselves "out." Their attempt at throwing a fit was, to be truthful, pathetic. So I asked Matt if he would be interested in teaching a unit on classic fit-throwing: its related benefits of tension release, the proper and safe way of throwing a fit, and, of course, the proper times for doing so. He calmly and matter-of-factly agreed to do so, stating his belief that such a skill was indeed lacking among his peers, all the while presenting the image of a miniature version of Spock (without the pointed ears).

In a couple of days, Spock, or rather Matt, said that he was prepared to present the lesson. After a short description of the "Classic Fit," an oration on its value to the child psyche and its importance on the playground, the class was escorted outside for the lab portion of the course.

Matt demonstrated for the class, in slow motion, the finer points of the Classic Fit as he had personally developed them over time and experience. He then ran the students through a couple of group fits as he instructed, corrected, and guided the proper technique.

Satisfied, he led the class back into the classroom. I followed and only then realized that we were in full view of three other classes. Almost one hundred students and three teachers stood in awed silence with their noses plastered against the windows of those classrooms as I walked back to my class. I smiled and nodded to them, thinking to myself, "Let them figure that one out!"

Needless to say, Classic Fit Throwing became the rage of the school and little Matt was the one to see for proper instruction on the safe and socially acceptable way to throw a fit after you tried so hard at a game and got put "out."

"I feel much better now."

Chapter 8
Poet And Don't Know It

"Today there is a problem of mine,

I can't behold a thing but rhyme," was my first (and challenging) statement of the day as I unlocked the door to the classroom.

"What? What do you mean . . . ?" came a reply from the group of various colored heads waiting to enter the class.

"I'm sorry, your words are unclear,

they do not rhyme unto my ear."

"Oh, I get it," piped another voice, upon entering the room, "the everyday strain of dealing with us kids has caused massive cerebral damage to our beloved teacher's cortex."

"What a pity," another chimed in, "let's hope it is only temporary or a gradual metamorphosis at worst. There's still aways to go in the school year." Such was to impress upon me that, yes, they do remember the vocab from our study on the brain, not to mention the unit on insects. Therefore the use of the word "metamorphosis"—hmm, was there a slanderous hint about my personality hidden in that comment?

"Yes, if only he can last until the end of the semester before he becomes so geriatric that we must commit him to a senior citizen retirement center . . ." (and we remember the study we did on aging . . .)

"We will choose a good one, of course. One with high walls, but no barbed wire so he won't hurt himself when he tries to escape and come to class."

It had begun. The banter of superior minds to the exclusion of the feeble and inferior one—mine. Next I feared they would lead me by the hand to the couch behind my desk, command me (firmly but gently) to recline my decrepit frame and rest from the exertions of the day (opening the door) and try, please, not to think. My worst fears were realized—I was led to the couch . . .

From the couch my voice arose, in verse: "Alas, rest all your fears, my little dears, I will soon be feeling fine, with just a little bit of rhyme, to soothe my ears."

The signal was caught, the "game was afoot," and I was not about to be let off the hook—wait a minute! This was to be my game. How did I get caught? to myself I thought.

"Did you notice an affliction—"

"A sort of dereliction;" ("Groan," thought I, "I've created a monster.")

"Yes, we'll call it an affliction,"

"And possibly a type of twitchin',"

"That has happened to our teacher, or uh, uh." The fifth line composer was at a loss to add his line to the verse, whereupon a lively discussion ensued about true verse and poetic license.

So began the unit on poetry that most members of the class had been unanimously opposed to. Of course, the "Write-in" books helped to loosen that set of minds a bit with its offer of an occasional poem for rewording. But all in all, poetry was not considered a favorite topic of study until now.

Class had begun 45 minutes before the first bell, and as "latecomers" arrived they joined the mania of verse and poem, meter, beat, rhyme and time; for teacher (the bigger person in the class) had this problem: he could only speak in rhyme.

Some of the worst poetry the world has ever witnessed was versed that day, which slowly grew into stuff that was tolerable, if not amusing. E.g.: "I think I thunk of a thought!" was at one time commented. Whereupon, the retort echoed back, "The thought you think you thunk, stunk." As the tone became more serious, and the humor more subtle and challenging, writings began to hold depth and meaning beyond mere reports of history or science. Yes, regular written assignments for the day were done in verse, without my asking. They knew a good thing when they saw it, and even went so far as to turn the thumbscrews tighter, with rhyme to connect basic math problems together into, dare I say, poetry.

I must admit, presenting every lesson and every comment for the day in rhyme was most taxing and challenging for me. Even the few and rare times that discipline was needed it was done in rhyme! Which I believe is even more effective . . . But I must give that more thought, and experimentation.

What made this poetic lesson so challenging was that I did not plan it. Those rhyming words, as I unlocked the door that morning, simply came out of my mouth. I'm sure such was inspired by a novel I was reading at home of the humorous trials and adventures of a 17th century poet. As it was, two things may have saved me: the fact that I was somewhat of an amateur poet during my early college years did help a little. More so was the fact that I was as much taken off guard as the class was about the necessity of speaking in rhyme, and almost as much of a novice as they. The key in this instance is the word "almost," for I had some experience to draw upon that put me at an only slight advantage over the class, not one that was beyond challenging or even overcoming by its members.

As it was, those who harbored a poet within recognized that element and allowed it to emerge, without threat or insurmountable competition from me. The poet within first peeked out, later emerged in glory, and was to stay, hopefully, for a lifetime.

While a few laureates emerged unto their own, others recognized a new and different way to encounter, appreciate, and announce the beauty of their thoughts and the world around them. Others simply had fun.

I was forced to admit, as upon that couch I did sit, here there were better poets than I. I accept this defeat, oh gloriously I am beat!

Postscript: The poetry never stopped from that day on. Oh, it did taper off and I was excused for not speaking in rhyme on other days (due to "geriatric affliction of a gradual metamorphose syndrome"—advancing old age), but the magic that touched the heart was forever there. And from time to time I was to have such beautiful writings of feelings and upliftment shared with me from those poet laureates, so much more masterful than I. "Oh glorious defeat am I . . ."

Chapter 9

AAAs . . . And Secretaries

"This is a great paper you've written," I was saying to a shy and quiet student as we sat on the couch behind my desk. "Your report is excellent and twice as long as was required."

The reason I wasn't sitting at my desk is that one of my two "secretaries" was using it to grade spelling papers and to enter the grades in the grade book. These secretaries that I "hired" for two-week jobs allowed me time from mundane tasks (I didn't need to learn those spelling words, they did, and after correcting 35 or so tests, they knew those words thoroughly and loved it. They actually thought it was fun!). So I had time to spend on one-to-one personal encounters with each student on a regular basis.

Often as not this individual attention was spent in pleasant talk about feelings and needs, social situations and skills, or just some quiet time spent sitting together reading, doing class work, or discussing projects and assignments, as I was doing with this child. It was a pleasant and relaxing experience.

Since her paper was twice as long as required and of "A" quality, I just couldn't justify awarding such effort with only one "A." So I gave it two "A"s. She was quite pleased, to say the least, and I sensed a motivation growing within her that was lacking before. The entire class would soon experience this increased motivation brought on by this "multiple grade" system. It virtually eliminated doing only the required amount of work, because one would still get the same grade for a little as a lot (since grades were awarded for quality and not quantity). Now one got "paid" not just for the quality of work, but also for the quantity. Weeks later, after much hard work, this same student turned in a fifteen page research paper (yes, the class had learned how to do research that would make some college students blush) that was worthy of being used for a science unit presentation. So that is what I did. Years later she visited her old class and asked if I was still using her paper for that science unit. I told her yes, and that she was credited as the author. The spark in her eye grew just a little bit brighter.

Having been a student in my early years of elementary education who did not know what an "A" on a paper looked like, except for on another, "smarter" kid's paper, I knew what such a feeling was like. It was a downer. Debilitating, degrading and destructive down to the marrow of the bone. I was not about to allow that to happen in my class to my kids.

"Hey, this is a great paper you've written." I was saying (on the couch again) to a student who knew only what the lower grades on papers looked like. The smooth curve of a gentle "C" was the lowest grade I gave. If the paper wasn't awarded a "C," then it was awarded a comment to the likes of, "You've got a good start here—see me for some pointers and we'll make it better."

He said, "Yeah, but not as good as some papers from the smarter kids in the class."

I answered by saying, "It's the best you've turned in so far, and as far as I'm concerned it's an "A" paper. I also learned a lot from what you wrote about, thanks." The lone tear and the smile that came revealed his confusion as to which was better, the grade or the fact that a student, who only knew low grades, was actually smart enough to teach the teacher something of value.

Now I would never admit to setting up a "sting." It was never suspected that I would arrange the topic to match the interest and abilities, or manipulate the attitudes in order to build a fire under the seat of an unsuspecting person many years my junior. Not me. I'm not that kind of underhanded, conniving person, I'm worse. I let others do my "dirty" work by subtly placing ideas geared to stimulate underhanded and conniving thoughts and plans. One of my secretaries plotted this sting. She came up with the idea, after a little bit of, shall we say, help, from ideas or mumblings of a slightly confused and sometimes bumbling teacher (who was overworked, often distracted, and sometimes prone to thinking out loud).

This secretary and I were going over the grade book together for my verification of her work, which was impeccable. She knew she would train her replacement, as she was so trained, and she did not want any mistakes tarnishing her reputation. As we reviewed the grades of the particular student in question, I commented, as I arose to help a student at his desk, "I sure wish I could think of a situation to help this boy get an 'A' on something. Can you think of anything sneaky?" I was skilled in subtlety, circumlocution of a point, beating around the bush . . .

When I returned she said, "Yes, I've thought of an idea. Listen carefully and try to pay attention."

She said, "He needs the encouragement of an 'A' on a paper, I know. He lives near me and we play together sometimes. He's afraid to try because he thinks he's dumb. Well, he is (kid honesty!), but not in everything. He loves motorcycles and knows a lot about the different kinds of racing bikes. He really is smart. If we could get him to . . ." The plot was born.

As it turned out, that was not the last "A" he ever received. With the help of another teacher, unbeknownst to that teacher, he was to accelerate even further. This is the story as he reported it to me:

Time: just after recess.

"I just saw Mrs._____, my old fourth grade teacher, and I told her that I got an 'A+' on a paper. And she said there was no such thing as an 'A+.'"

I just sat there, thinking of that teacher arranging the bun of hair at the back of her head.

"I said, 'Yes there is! I got an 'A+' on my paper.' Then Michelle, from our class, told her that she got two 'A's on one paper! Mrs. _____ just made a huffing sound and went into her classroom. Do you think that I could ever get two 'A's on a paper?"

"I expect you to do so any time now," said I, thinking to have him do a report on motorcycle mechanics next. He didn't see the tear that was trying to squeeze out of the corner of my eye as I gripped the cushion of the couch and all but pushed a pillow into my mouth to keep from howling with laughter. That teacher really did wear her hair in a bun!

A comment came from across the class, "You're plotting something! I can tell by the look on your face!" (Curses, caught again.)

Chapter 10

More On Secretaries

"It's true," I was saying to the two students interviewing for the secretary position. "During the two weeks that you work as secretaries, you get automatic 'A's for all assignments and you do not even have to do them."

This sounded better than it actually was. It was only single "A"s that were granted, and any student could earn extra on most assignments. Actually, they only thought they didn't have to do any assignments. Go ahead, accuse me of being sneaky, I deserve it. Before any secretary could grade a paper, say for history, they would have to read the chapter in the text and the quiz questions for the open-book quiz, and understand both. Then, by the time as many as 30 plus essay quizzes were read through, and consultations were made with the students who wrote those papers and/or with me . . . Actually, I don't see why anybody would want such a position.

There were benefits, though. The secretaries got to use my desk on a regular basis, and they actually got paid in marks for their effort. They also were responsible for reminding the class of time. This seems like a rather minor thing to be a necessity, but somehow the classroom clock on the wall stopped working. There were rumors that the insides had mysteriously disappeared. I found that hard to believe. Why would anyone wish to do something like that? And since I never thought to look at my watch, well, somebody had to keep track of time or we could end up forgetting to go home at the end of the day.

Part of the secretary's job description was greeting visitors when they arrived and explaining our class and how it functioned. Such a chore could easily take a full hour just for the basics. As social directors/tour guides it was up to the secretaries to evaluate the interest and needs of the individual visitor, and decide how best to satisfy them.

We had a lot of visitors, because somehow we received a lot of publicity. I suspect that some of the parents were occasionally calling the press to expose our interesting classroomology. Sneaky. An interested visitor could easily spend an entire day having the integral structure explained as he or she was passed from one classroomology expert to another, from the secretaries to the manager or owner of the bank or the class store, and sometimes even to the board of directors and investors at such times when the class itself was owned and managed by a corporation. The interested visitor would be passed from person to person for a most in-depth experience.

The Community Work Experience program could take an hour or more alone to explain. The tutor program, the office help program, and numerous other concepts and experiments both past and present needed explaining to the brave visitor possessing the stamina to withstand the onslaught of information.

There were times, as generally was the rule, when I only briefly met the visitor before they were whisked away to the "authority" of a certain aspect of the class. But that was okay; I was busy with more "sneaky" ideas and one-to-one contact. There were times when I didn't speak with the visitor at all, except for a brief introduction at the arrival and a dazed "thank you" at the end of their visit. "Who was that person?" I would sometimes need to ask. "Oh, that was the president of the school board," came the secretary's reply. "Hmm, seemed like a nice person," I said. "Did he get a good tour?" "The standard," came the reply. "I told him that you thought the school board was unnecessary and dumb . . ." "You what?!" I almost shouted. "Just kidding, just kidding. It's almost time for P.E. and I checked to see if the gym is free, it is. Could we play volleyball?" "Sure, sure, the gym's not free that often . . ." Boy, you really know how to wake a guy up.

"Wait a minute! There is never any problem this time of day with using the gym, of course it's free. Hey! Wait a minute, we've played volleyball for the last two days."

Too late, duped again. When did I lose control around here?

Chapter 11

Tell Me, How Do You Tie A Shoelace?

Well, that's easy enough. Everybody knows how to tie a shoelace. You don't even have to think about it. Such were the general thoughts of the class members as they read that particular assignment in their weekly assignment packet.

This packet included various assignments, usually results of my moments of insanity as Mr. Hyde, bad dreams, wild inspirations, a mean streak, or just plain pay-back for some "underhanded" but creative prank played on me earlier. This is where one may find the art assignment to draw the back of one's own head, to prove that the California Gold Rush was a hoax played out by the real estate agents of that era, to find a way to prove that one plus one does not necessarily make two, or what is the weight of your hand, without removing it from your arm! And, for this particular week: "My shoelace comes untied sometimes and I would like to have written directions telling me exactly how to tie it. You know how I sometimes forget things. Thank you for your help."

The assignment seemed quite simple, but the class had not quite caught on that some of the most "simple" things in everyday life can be the most difficult—and most important—and that what may appear to be the most difficult can turn out to be the most simple—and sometimes the least important.

Now, I could have been really mean and asked the students to describe the sound of a violin as you would to a deaf person, or describe the color orange to a blind person. Another slice of reality indeed—as I found out the time that I was a tutor for a visually-impaired person.

Of course, I wasn't that mean, and certainly not to a bunch of kids, at least not until they learned how to tie a shoelace, on paper . . . such meanness I was holding for next week! Ha, ha! I'll show the little monsters. I'll show them that they better not mess with me and that they can do anything they put their little minds to! The latter they learned, we both did, but they never did learn not to mess with me. That remained too much fun and too much of a challenge—a challenge by which we all did quite well.

Chapter 12

With Your Permission, May I Tell You A Lie?

"Some of what you are told, taught, or hear in life will be incomplete information, partially untrue, or totally wrong. Some will be outright lies." Everybody in the class could easily accept this statement, since they had enough experience with the "real" world to understand this concept. Almost. What they were not prepared to accept was my next statement: "And that goes for in here as well."

"What!?" was the general consensus of alarm, "But what you teach us is true. Isn't it?"

"Yes," I said, "as far as I know it is." And this was followed by a short discussion of "facts" that were once taught as truth: the earth is flat, or that it is impossible for a man (a woman wasn't even considered) to fly or go to the moon.

"Hmm," I thought, "when are they going to comment on the lie part?" And in the next breath, "What about the lie part?" a voice said. I answered, "Have you ever been lied to?" Of course the answer was yes. "Well, that is something I will never do to you here. I will always tell you the truth, to the best of my knowledge.

"Now, this is not to say that I can't be sneaky, or can't ever surprise you by creating situations that will help you learn and be fun to boot (boy, did they ever underestimate that one—'trick or treat' by Mr. Hyde!), but I will never intentionally lie to you, unless . . ." I allowed my voice to drop off—the challenge.

"Unless what?" said the fish, nibbling at the bait.

"Unless, I have your permission," said the fisherman. "But," I said, "you are going to be busy enough just questioning some of what I tell you and checking the facts out for yourself because some of what I will be teaching you is going to be hard to believe, and to have me feeding you a lie from time to time . . ."

The discussion at that point began to get interesting. Well, "interesting" is an understatement. The discussion ball was in their court and I was all but requested to be quiet while they discussed and debated the issue of honesty vs. "unhonesty," a very important part of their real world.

It was finally agreed that I had their permission to tell them three lies, fabrications, or untruths during the semester. The "misinformation," as we termed it, was to be in the form of a scientific fact. That is, a hoax. If I succeeded, which they doubted, I could gloat over them and strut back and forth for a whole minute in front of the class. If they caught me in the process or soon found me out (we didn't want the "fact" to be learned and remembered as truth), they could do the same. Of course, they would have to provide the proof to expose my hoax, which meant constant attention to the validity of everything they were told or taught, and, of course, a lot of research.

I was asking them simply (an understatement, to be honest) to become self-learners, self-motivated, and self-trusting. I didn't want them to believe something just because someone of "authority," "position," or "learning" said it was so. These people can be, and often are, in error through innocence or "not so innocence."

The class felt that I would not lie to them in the classic sense. Our relationship and character as a whole, our integrity, would never allow for it. It was possible for me to be wrong about something, or for the information I presented to be in error.

And the possibility of my pulling a fast one on them was always expected. They were used to double checking the information I presented in class, and a few times I had to correct my notes. They learned that there were no answers—only more questions. They found out every one of my hoaxes but one, and I got to strut for one whole minute.

Hmm—

I was once one of two head teachers for a special state program. My co-teacher was a delightful and energetic woman who was then experiencing her children as teenagers. Each morning before school we would hold a meeting with our aides and she would often begin by telling us some interesting and often humorous little story about her experiences raising teenagers.

One morning, as she told us of an experience she had just recently had, I soon realized that I was hearing the wisdom of the ages. It went like this:

"The other day, after I got home from school, my teenage daughter said to me, 'Mom, I think I'll shave half my head and dye the other side orange.' I was shocked and could think of no answer other than to simply say, 'Hmm.' Later my daughter came to me and said, 'I don't think I'll do that.' Once again I could only say, 'Hmm.' It was then that I realized just how perfect of an answer that was."

I realized the truth in her statement and have used this wonderful "answer" numerous times, and it has never failed to work. First of all, it gives one time to step back a bit from the situation. "Hmm," doesn't even have to be expressed out loud—and in some situations it is best to keep it silent. "Hmm," allows one to pause before one reacts, to not immediately buy into the drama in which the lives of youngsters can so often be involved. "Hmm," allows me to say, "Maybe that person knows what they're talking about and maybe not. Maybe I'll accept that program or maybe I won't."

"Hmm," does not reject or judge, nor does it agree—it simply accepts that what is there is there. Hmm.

Chapter 13

No Homework, If . . .

I hate homework. As a child in school I invariably forgot to do it, or rushed through it and did a poor or incomplete job. Why? Because I had just spent the greater part of the day in school and I wanted to play! Silly question. Homework caused problems for me at home. It interrupted important family times and I got in trouble for it more often than not. My hatred of homework didn't help my attitude towards school, towards home, or towards myself.

"I will never give you homework," were my profound words on the first day of each new school year. "Hooray," the cheer would begin from the crowd. "You will give it to yourself," I continued in the silence that followed, "if you do not keep up with your work in class." Easy enough for all to accept. They thought, "We'll keep up with classwork, no homework, no homework!"

What I didn't tell them was that they would find their studies so interesting that they would actually ask if they could take work home. A silly question, for one could simply do so whether permission was granted or not. But of course I always gave my permission after cautioning against letting such work interfere with family time or play. Such was a true concern on my part, and I believe it was truly appreciated on the child's part. Love is expressed in many ways.

Sometimes parents expressed concern over the absence of homework: "My child never brings work home—says you don't give homework—hard to believe—how can anything be achieved without homework?—learning must be painful not fun . . ." Whereupon I would display the volume of work produced in class by the student: "My child did all that? That's amazing."

The other end of the spectrum was: "The amount of work my child brings home is staggering. Is she not doing anything in class? Is that why she has so much homework?" After a few reassurances, I asked if the child was reluctant, dissatisfied, or feeling pressured about the work brought home.

Answer: "No, not in the least. Voracious would be a better term." Ah, my ears detected sweet chomping sounds of knowledge being gobbled up. I then inquired if this voracity interfered with play life or family life, hoping upon hope that such was not so.

Answer: "Yes," (a slight gulp from me) "but in a most encouraging and delightful way. The whole family is involved and is most interested in the various projects." (Cancel that gulp, I was confident all along.) "I must say, you are employing some rather unique techniques, off-the-wall, to be frank. (Another gulp). What you're doing is great," (cancel the other gulp) "thank you." Then the words were uttered; the words I love to hear, the words I waited for: "If there is anything I can do to help . . ." Music to my ears? The music of Richard Strauss' "Dawn" (the theme of the movie "2001, A Space Odyssey") burst upon me and, I, Jekyll, calmly and elegantly replied, "Well, now that you mention it, there is a little something you could help with. Our class could use some materials. Things like 2 x 4s, plywood, carpet scraps, furniture, but only if you happen to have them lying around the home and in the way. We could also use a few appliances . . ."

Chapter 14
The View From On Top Of The Desk

"This is a very important point to remember," I was saying to the class. "It is the key to understanding what we are presently studying."

I was addressing the class from the top of my desk. No, not from the corner of the desk where I often perched myself, in a seated position while talking to the class. I was standing on my desk, and I had their undivided attention. They were at my mercy; they would never forget the day the teacher stood on his desk. And, I hoped, they would never forget the all-important point that I wanted them to remember.

The main reason for such behavior on my part was that I sensed that I did not have enough of their intellectual awareness for the concept to sink in. So, I sunk it in. Such "shock therapy" (I like the term "off-the-wall") can be very effective if it isn't overdone. Twice a year was my limit for standing on my desk—at least while the class was present. The perspective is quite nice from up there, no wonder the kids liked the upper levels of the high-rise sections of the class.

So if I only stood on my desk twice a year, it was necessary to have a repertoire of "off-the-wall" shockers or attention-getters for use at the proper times. The Groucho glasses and nose, with bushy eyebrows and mustache, were good for a few times, an excellent imitation of Donald Duck's voice, a certain humorous Halloween mask, all worked wonders on the right occasion. A life-size rubber chicken ("dead" and plucked) just casually held or made to dance to the rhythm of an important point to remember;

"What was the point the chicken made?" I could later ask. Numerous impromptu props, words, and actions all served to wake up, stimulate, humor, and most of all, create a warm and receptive rapport. If they remembered the important point—well, that was good, too.

By the way, these exact same attention shockers work just as well with adult students (big kids) and are possibly even more appreciated by them.

Chapter 15

Free Time—You Can Buy It!

The concept of earning free time, that is, time off from class studies and work during a school day, was certainly a unique concept for a child to consider.

"You mean to tell us," said one child, during one of our informal class discussions, "that for a certain amount of marks I can actually buy free time? To do whatever I wish? To work in the mechanics workshop, read, draw or paint or even go outside and play? While everyone else is working?"

"Yes," I said, "as long as you are caught up with your work and have proven yourself to be a self-responsible individual," a concept that was of the highest priority in our class.

"Of course," she said, essentially stating that I needn't even mention the obvious.

"You could, for example, buy an hour of free time—well, right now, if you wish to . . ."

"Not now!" I could almost hear the word "dummy" or "silly" added to her comment, "I don't want to miss out on our discussion."

Murmurs and comments of "yeah," or "really," or "no way," came from various members of the class, signifying their desire to not miss out on the discussion.

"Whew," I thought to myself, "no takers," and I braced myself mentally for what I was about to say. I didn't exactly know just what it was I was about to say, but I knew my tendency to stretch a good thing for all its worth, push to the limit . . . and sure enough, it came: "You could even save your marks and buy a number of hours of free time if you wanted to!" (Wait! Did I just say what I thought I heard myself say?)

Well, at least I didn't say a whole day—and there it was, ". . . or a whole day of free time!" (to be spent at school, of course—not to mention the obvious).

Like Britain's Parliament, the murmurs and comments of the class increased in volume at that last statement, so that my following comment—muttered somewhat under my breath, of, "You may also wish to tie me up and throw rubber erasers at me as well," was only heard by one of my secretaries who was standing close by me. She took hold of my arm and hugged it saying, "Could we shoot rubber bands at you, too?" with a big grin on her face.

Secretaries were used to hearing the mutterings of my mental ravings and would often as not use them for a little bit of humor. Such as, "Did you wish for me to announce that to the class?" in a most innocent and sweet little voice.

And I might respond, in a sweet and menacing voice, "Would you like me to bend some of your fingers the wrong way?" Whereupon, as likely as not, said secretary would make motions to make such announcement—whereupon I would follow up my threat by saying, "Uh, no thank you, uh, please do not make the announcement just yet. Thank you for your offer to help . . ." (When did I lose control?)

"Would you bend my fingers anyway? I like the sound—like pretzels snapping," may well come the retort.

"You are a very sick little person. Do you realize that?" going back to my mumbling, but in a lower tone.

"Yes, thank you. I enjoy having a twisted mind, it gives me satisfaction to be able to think in alternative ways from the acceptable standard norm. Creative geniuses are often different, according to my research on that subject . . ." The dialogue would continue. All this from the mouth (and brain) of a child? I continued to mumble to myself, as I looked over some test papers.

"Do you think I could be a creative genius?" she continued, "I think that may be a distinct possibility from what I've read on the subject."

"I believe that is quite possible, my dear. Here, grade these papers—the ability to do this task will undoubtedly prove that you have some aspect of genius in you. Such a task is beyond me."

"Yes, I understand. Do you mind if I eat my pretzels at the same time?" And realizing that I was ignoring her, she smiled and added, "Or my eraser?"

I sat there and thought to myself, "Maybe if I ate erasers it would stop my mumblings, or at least cause them to be unintelligible." No, the fact is I wouldn't miss these encounters of witty bantering for anything. I'll continue to mutter the ravings of my mind.

"I'm going to save my marks and buy a whole day off!" That and similar comments from the class served to bring me back to the reality of the here and now. They were raring to go—a whole day off! Wow! Pour on the work, extra credit, research projects, anything at all, something to sink their teeth into! Requests came for the "Draw a Project" box. This was a concept I had thought of for extra credit assignments and research projects. The box contained over 2,000 topics that reports could be done from, each one written on a 2-inch by 2-inch square of paper and worth a certain value according to the degree of difficulty. I had to write them all by myself—not being able to think of any way to bribe the secretaries into it.

"I hope I draw 'nuclear physics' or something like that," came one voice, "that should be worth a lot! I know I can do it, even if I have to call up the nearest nuclear reactor station . . ."

As it turned out, only one person ever purchased a full day off. And then he kept coming back to the classroom from the library or the playground in order not to miss anything interesting that might have been going on. He spent most of his time interacting in class, but from a different perspective; more like a freelance participant, almost like an outsider to his own "family." I watched with interest and realized that my impromptu decision was going to work out just fine. Things were just too interesting in the class to be left out. And I had better keep it so.

"It really feels weird to be the only kid on the playground while the whole school is in class. It gave me time to do a lot of thinking," he was to tell me later. So we sat down on the sofa behind my desk; I asked my secretaries to please take over (and no pretzel crumbs on the desk), and I said, "So tell me, what did you think about out there on the playground all alone?" I was in a mood to learn.

The first unit I taught each year was a very explicit, thorough, and extensive study of: whole food nutrition vs. the Standard American Diet (SAD), junk food vs. real food, common sense eating vs. non-thinking or compulsive eating, etc., etc.

Some of the greatest changes I have ever seen in children, took place as a direct result of improved nutrition. These were improved attention span, eliminated hyperactivity, greater self–esteem, positive outlook on life, enhanced ability to concentrate, contemplate, think, etc., etc. Just real foods—not drugs.

We changed the old saying of GIGO (garbage in, garbage out) to QIQO (quality in, quality out). Makes sense.

Chapter 16

The Project Box

The Project Box. Over 2,000 topics to choose from. That's a lot. Some are easy, some are hard. The easy ones are worth less than the hard ones. There are supposed to be some real hard ones in the box that are worth a lot—if you can do them. Nobody has ever picked one of those yet.

You get to draw three times if you want to, but the last time you have to keep what you pick, and if it's a real hard one—well, you can do it if you really try.

It's almost like a quiz or a game show on TV. Like a studio audience, the class is watching as you pick the first piece of paper from the box with a subject title and its value written on it. They're hoping, along with you, that you will pick one that you'll like. Actually, I don't think anyone has really picked one they just couldn't stand. I know that I haven't.

The first topic is picked. Everybody holds back a breath—"Reptiles." Worth 35 marks. I decide to pick again and the class agrees. We already studied reptiles and I feel I know enough about them at this time. I want something more challenging. I almost wish I would pick one of the real hard ones—no, not really—well, actually, yes. I know I could do it.

My second draw from the box is "telephone service, long distance," worth 100 marks. That's a good price and not a bad subject. 100 marks for a full, one-page report of "A" quality—less if only "B" quality and much less if "C" quality. Of course the amount could be doubled if the report size and content information is doubled. Wordiness alone doesn't count, of course.

I hesitate and consider if this is what I'm really looking for. Some in the class say take it—only one more chance and maybe the last pick (the one I have to keep) will be yucky. Others say pick again! They're curious to see what the last one may be. The excitement grows.

I calm my mind and block out the urgings of others. I can make up my own mind according to what I feel is right for me at this time. We've talked about that a number of times in class discussions.

I decide to pick again. I want something more interesting. If I draw a topic that is too easy, I'll just do it and then pick again until I get what I want.

OK, here goes, the last and final pick. The class is silent as the box is shaken—I think mostly to add a little extra drama to the whole thing. We've all learned long ago that our teacher requires an alert and watchful eye on him at all times—he is full of surprises. And right this moment he has a look about him that tells me he might be up to something. Could I be on Candid Camera? I wouldn't put anything past him. Probably he is going to offer to double the price of whatever I pick if I write the report in the style that a newspaper reporter would use. He offered that last week to someone who took him up on it, and the kid actually called the newspaper to see if he could interview a news reporter to learn his style of writing. It worked, and now this kid writes half his work as though he is a foreign correspondent. Maybe I could beat him to the punch and do the report in Chinese!

I pull out a square of paper from the box. It's folded in half, as usual, and I slowly open it and begin to read. The class is getting anxious and already there are four kids waiting beside me to pick a project. This is extra credit and you must be caught up with all your regular class work in order to qualify. But that's no problem for most of us.

"Describe the process of opening a savings account at a bank." Worth 150 marks. Well, it's not one of the real biggies, but it sounds interesting. I already know how I'm going to go about it: I'm going to open a savings account at a bank, but I have a feeling it's going to take more than one page to explain the process.

Later, as I sit at my desk, a plan begins to form in my head. Actually, it's a plot. He's sitting on the couch behind his desk writing, probably a new brainstorm; one secretary is proofing papers at his desk, the other is helping another kid with math problems. It's fun being a secretary. It's also a lot of work.

A couple of months ago I worked at the bank in town for our Community Work Experience Program. The manager was real nice. I bet he would be willing to visit the class and talk about how an account is opened . . . no, that's not good enough. Maybe if he came in and I interviewed him like a reporter would do? No. Maybe I could open a savings account at the bank first and then do the whole process again in class? The bank president did say that if he could ever be of assistance . . . Look at him. He's grinning, and full of plans for us, as he sits there writing. I just know he's planning something! I think I'll sign up to work at the bank again, heh, heh, heh. The Bank of Hong Kong has a branch in a nearby city—a little bit of Chinese can't be that hard to learn. . .

Chapter 17
Turkey Feast

Twice each year parents would provide a turkey feast for the whole class. These wonderful patron saints of delicious food and yummy deserts fluttered into our classroom on silver wings and with halos of gold early in the morning on the day of the planned event.

These saint-like parents would bring all the fixings of a turkey feast that would feed a class of seventy little angels. Since we didn't have any angels in the class, thirty-five gremlins, disguised and acting like angels, ate enough for seventy. Each gremlin ate at least twice his or her weight in food. But I figured that since they produced about twice as much work as any average student, they deserved twice the food. Of course, if one considered that they also worked three or four times as hard at trying to keep one step ahead of me during the course of any given day, the argument could be presented that they be allowed to make total gluttons of themselves. Something none of us, of course, would ever do.

The parents took charge and turned the classroom into a kitchen. They presented a half-day crash course on feast preparation, and three dozen miniature chefs were orchestrated into producing a symphony of washed, prepared and decorated cooked–to–perfection food. It was delicious. Needless to say that we all made total gluttons of ourselves.

Having been a professional cook at one time in my distant past, I had the philosophy that food preparation and cleanliness go hand in hand. I could tell that some of this philosophy must have rubbed off during the course of the semester by comments I overheard: "He always washes his hands before he eats," and "If he drops food on the floor, it gets washed."

One such conversation went like this:

"I saw him wash his sandwich once and he didn't even drop it!"

"Really?"

"Yeah. He used soap on it, too."

"Come on, no way."

"Ask him if you don't believe me."

When asked, I of course said that I did do just that with a sandwich, but that it was a total disaster. The sandwich was peanut butter and jelly, and it wasn't so much the soap as the scrub brush I used that made an inedible mess out of it.

This was solely a distraction technique on my part. For while they were laughing at the mental image of the sandwich being scrubbed, I managed to snatch a couple pieces of the food they were preparing. I had been maneuvering around the classroom performing such sleight–of–hand tricks in order to obtain various bits of food in practice for the main event of gorging. Until now I had been doing quite well. This time I was spotted by a third party and was obliged to bribe this fellow glutton's mouth shut with part of my booty.

Actually, I had been caught almost every time, but the bribe technique never failed to work. In the guild of gluttonous food snatchers there is a strict code of silence through sharing. Our secret password is "Yum."

Chapter 18

The Value Of Solitude

I once taught at a very special private school. The teachers were special, the kids were special, and the subjects experienced in this small school, nestled in a green valley, were also special.

The property of the school consisted of a fair amount of secluded acreage. There was on this peaceful acreage a wooden tower, built at one time by those of past classes. It was called a tower, but was actually an open deck on tall stilt legs, with a shade roof of wood, about ten feet square. It was quiet, solitary and peaceful at the tower. Often after school or dinner (for my wife and I lived on the school property), I would walk to the tower and enjoy the beauty of the sunset, the quiet and the solitude. I would sit in the tower and think and relax.

I thought to myself: how could I share this state of quietness with my students? Have they before experienced such a meditative state? They do come out to the tower during the day, but not for solitude and quiet. Has any one of them ever spent a whole day in solitude—voluntary solitude? Not speaking or hearing another voice?

We discussed this idea in class one day and it wasn't too long after that, early one morning, just before class, that a boy asked if it would be alright for him to spend the day in solitude, in the tower. I knew that he had some important things in his life to think about. And the time was right for him to do it.

I agreed, explained some basic rules for safety, and made some suggestions to ensure his solitude would not be interrupted by others.

The preparations were quickly made and off he went with wishes of wellness from his classmates, and lunch and water in hand.

From time to time I would look out of the classroom window that day at the tower in the distance with the lone figure sitting, standing, lying or leaning on the rail. I would wonder, "How are you doing out there all alone? Was there enough food in your sack lunch for your body? Is there enough food for thought for your twelve-year-old mind?" It was a long day for me that day. It was a long day for all of us in class.

From time to time one of the kids would look towards the tower. "Is he still there?" came the question from another child at his or her seat. "Yeah, he's still there—sitting down."

Later in the day another child would question the one looking at the tower, "What's he doing?" The answer, "I think he's eating his lunch." And later: "What's he doing now?" "Looks like he's peeing over the side—hard to tell." Good, I thought, he's probably drinking enough water.

To say that things went as usual on that day would be untrue. It was to be a day that would stand alone in time, in the memories of each one of our minds, just as that boy had stood in that tower, a lone figure in the distance against the clear sky. We all felt his solitude even though we were together, a small group in a classroom. We could feel his thoughts, his need to be alone, his quietness. It affected us all in a way that is difficult to describe—it was like a quiet sadness but a good kind of sadness; the kind that helps you to think, to reflect upon your life and who you are.

The day, like all days, ended. A long

call from one of his classmates and the quiet figure in the tower climbed down and started walking back in our direction.

He wore an almost beatific smile of peace on his face; a quietness, but with less sadness in it.

I said, "How was it?" And he answered, "It was good—it was good. Thanks." And with shirt in hand headed for the car and parent that would take him home.

Insubordination

Insubordination happens when communication is absent and self-respect is out to recess. The results are embarrassing; everybody loses and feelings feel like they're doing detention.

When a person is insubordinate towards another because they are upset, angry or frustrated, they have temporarily given their power away. That's right—when you lose your temper, when you get angry, out of control, and act out of frustration by being insubordinate towards another, you have just given away your power, your control, to that other person. In short, you have just lost. Whether you were right or wrong to begin with, you become the loser. This is not only embarrassing and belittling, but is unnecessary and unfair to oneself.

All too often kids become losers when they should be winners, simply because they are unable to communicate, do not have the opportunity to communicate, or give up and will not communicate.

When people take the time to give an honest effort to talk and work towards understanding each other, nobody loses and everybody wins; no conflict continues and no wars begin.

Kids can learn to communicate in order to solve their problems. When we solve our problems by sensible means, we are doing something many heads of state and leaders of countries often seem to be unable to do—and that's something to be proud of—really proud. Kids' communication = kids' power = kids' pride!

Chapter 19

Community Work Experience Program

How many kids can boast of having worked in as many as 15 to 20 different businesses in their community during a school year? I would have parents tell me how interesting it was to spend time shopping with their son or daughter because, "He (she) knows everybody in every store or business we go to, it seems like!" Kids who encountered the Community Work Experience Program would proudly introduce their family members to business managers and employees and explain the "behind the scene" working of said establishment.

To begin this career education program, I first had to attain the consent of a number of local business owners. That meant I had to convince them that kids would be responsible enough to merit this person's, and his or her employees', time and effort. Actually, it meant that I had to place my personal word, professional reputation, and my life (if I was ever caught in their business) on the line if these kids were not everything, and more, than what I cracked them up to be. At least it seemed like that to me after I had "interviewed" 15 to 20 business owners. I say "interview" because while they thought they were interviewing me, I was more interested in what kind of people they were, what the general atmosphere of their establishment was, and what impact such would have on my kids. As far as my program being accepted by them, I felt pretty confident. As far as the kids living up to my verbal treatises of their wonderfulness and fantasticness . . . well, if they didn't I could probably move to some small, unknown town in Mexico.

So for part of the semester, every Tuesday and Thursday, automobiles would pull up to the front of the school, with a parent behind each wheel. Each vehicle would stop, receive a load of children, and drive away to deposit one pair of kids at each business on their particular route. In about an hour the procedure would be reversed and the groups of children would be returned to school.

Verbal reports would be given, with an excitement hard to contain, about the experience at a given workplace. Yes, they indeed did work there. Each child participated to the degree that the business was able to provide. That was the whole idea: hands on, not just a tour.

Kids learned to bag groceries, stock supplies and produce, visit the upstairs offices, and learn about two-way mirrors in the super market. They watched bank transactions from the inside of the teller cage and held piles of money in the vault. At the police and sheriff station they sat with the dispatcher, saw the jail, visited those back rooms the officers only see, and rode in the squad cars around the block.

Department stores, car dealers, machine shops, sporting goods stores, furniture stores, restaurants, hardware stores, medical and dental offices, public library, music store, hotel . . . so went the list.

The reports from the kids were quite favorable and encouraging. I didn't expect that they would let me, themselves, or the class down, and they didn't. I didn't really expect to move to Mexico. The kids themselves offered critiques and constructive criticism about how they could improve their behavior—that's why they went in pairs, to serve as a mirror for each other. After all, this was practice.

After a couple of visits I called or dropped by to talk to those people at the other end. Every report was favorable and continued to be so during the entire program. In fact, the praise and positive comments were greater than anyone expected. I was even told a couple of times that I didn't exaggerate at all about the responsibility of the kids (whew!). They were even better than some high school students who were visiting or working at certain businesses! Boy, did the class ever love to hear that.

Best of all was the change in the feeling of "can do," self-confidence, and self-responsibility in the class, and from the comments of many parents at home, there was noticeable change on that end, too. The class atmosphere took a shift in maturation and as a result I was (heh, heh, heh) able to put into practice some plans that had been forming in the back of "Mr. Hyde's" mind. To all indications, they were ready; the classroom began to dissolve before my eyes as I rubbed my gnarled hands together in anticipation. "Yes," I said to myself, "an idea is coming to me . . ."

"Look, you guys!" said a voice, rudely breaking into my scheming reverie. "He's planning something for us! You can see it in his eyes." My accuser was standing on the upper level of the balcony pointing her finger at me. Curses, caught again. I thought I was hidden from view, all slouched down into the couch behind my desk.

As a young man I painted custom cars as a part–time business. One old and wise mentor of the craft once told me something that stuck in my mind: "People think that painting a car is difficult. It's not. It's the preparation that takes skill, knowledge and hard work. Ninety-eight percent of the work is in the prep. The painting is easy.

"Go over all the details carefully, lovingly; do the best you can. And when you feel that it is ready, apply the finish and enjoy the results." Yes, I thought to myself, the finish is made all the more enjoyable by the preparation involved.

The Responsibility of Communication

Kids need to realize that they can be empowered through self-responsibility and that they can and should be involved in discussion and decision making.

An individual who is not a part of the communication and decision-making process, who is not heard and is expected to only listen, feels to be a part *from* rather than a part *of*. This person will lose or not develop the skills necessary to be included in such processes in the future. Such a person often tends to act against that system.

Adults and kids should meet with open minds and mutual respect. For many children, such may well be the first interaction of this kind in their lives. The benefits can be powerful and long-lasting.

Chapter 20

Squares Of The Wall For Sale

"Each square is priced at 100 marks," I was telling the class, "and you can draw the number that will be your square whenever you wish."

It was a simple class art project we were doing that took a little extra effort in group cooperation. I really wasn't selling pieces of the classroom wall—well, actually I was, but nothing that could be taken home—not that kind of ownership.

The sections of wall being sold were twelve inches square and were to be painted from a gridwork to form a finished project of a beautiful mural. This was my plan. This is not what happened, though. First of all, no one could agree on the scene for a mural; something we would all be looking at for a given period of time. Second, nobody was that interested in painting a 12-inch square of wall that was only a nonsense piece of a scene all by itself. Third, we soon realized that there was not enough bare wall space, unless we included the chalkboards, to use for anything but a puny painting. The whole inside of the building was needed and we had too many structures erected in the class to allow anything like that. Okay, so I didn't research this one very well!

I had gotten permission from the principal to do murals inside the classroom, just before he ran into his office the other day. We were calmly chatting out in front of the school as the kids were getting on the buses to go home. I mentioned how my kids were wanting to paint a mural they had seen in a magazine of a school's front building all done in bright cheerful colors—and how nice it would be if our school had more color to it . . .

I could tell he was getting nervous at what he thought I was about to propose by the way he was rubbing the back of his neck, and how he kept glancing back towards his office. It actually looked like he had to go potty the way he was beginning to pace around—and maybe he did, I don't know. Some people have to wet when they get too nervous.

I mentioned that probably the walls inside my classroom would be adequate to satisfy the "Michelangelo" urge of some of my students, and he readily agreed just before he hastily excused himself (maybe he did have to go) to run to his office, mumbling something about hearing his secretary calling him. I didn't hear anything, but then the buses were making a lot of noise just then.

As it turned out, the whole project of a group mural was a flop. The kids realized that I didn't do my homework on this one and proceeded to do what I should have done to start with. They took over, organized the information available, and began a process of deciding who would have the privilege of painting whatever they wished on pieces of the wall available. All real estate was dear, and that which is dear, and in demand, can be expensive! I could see that right away. If I was allowed to conduct the bidding (now that things were properly organized), I could well imagine it would be intent and furious. I could see co-ops, corporations, and agencies forming of power hungry, high finance bosses—collectives of buyers . . .

"We've decided that every person should be able to paint the bare wall space closest to his or her desk or work space. It's only fair, since that person, or persons, are the ones that have to live with it. If they don't do a good job, then they will be the ones who mainly have to look at it. Is that okay?" a spokesperson said to me.

Having been drawn rather abruptly from my fantasy, I quickly gathered my wits and regained control. I said, "Huh?" The spokesperson said, "Of course, no one will paint the area near your desk—you may do that if you wish."

"Good," I managed to say, still a little off balance.

"Okay, it's settled then," the spokesperson announced to the class.

"Did you plan it to work out like this?" came the accusation from someone. "Anyone can easily see that there is not enough wall space to do a class mural!"

"No, no, really I didn't. You guys did just fine. You made it work just right," I insisted, as I looked around to see if maybe the principal's secretary was calling me. Maybe I should go visit with him in his office—his nice safe office. Maybe I have to go potty.

Problem: People are afraid of what they don't understand.
Solution: Learn to understand (the challenge).

Chapter 21
My Box

"They're to kick, of course. What better use for a box when there is nothing to put in it?" I said as I unloaded the stack of various sized boxes in front of the classroom door.

"You mean, you brought these boxes just for us to kick? Really?" said one student.

Another chimed in, "He's such a thoughtful teacher. He realizes that we kids are stressed out and psychologically on the verge of having our mental, physical and emotional triangle disrupted into little teeny pieces from this week's art project, and has brought us boxes to work our frustrations out on . . ."

All this from the mouth of a child—where did I go wrong? I should never have presented anything to these little monsters regarding psychology, like the film on stress and the importance of balancing the three sides of the triangle for proper health.

"Is this our new art project for the week? Draw a box!?" another voice piped in. At this point I wasn't even looking at the little gremlins as I focused all my intelligence and abilities on the framing of a masterful and witty retort in order to demonstrate the superior intellect and wisdom that is achieved by age, experience and education: "Why won't that dumb key fit in the lock?" I said.

"Elementary, my dear Watson," said a ten-year-old mouth from the group of midgets amassed at the door, intermingling amongst the boxes, and patiently waiting to enter the classroom. "The key you are presently attempting to use in order to open the classroom door has a Ford Motor Company emblem on it. With the powers of my deductive reasoning, I presume it is your car key—since you do drive a Ford. Rather poor taste in motor cars, I should think."

"Would you like a hammer?"

"No I do not wish a hammer, Holmes." Never again will I discuss, in the presence of children, the concept of deductive reasoning or the phenomenon of Sherlock Holmes.

"What are the boxes for?" came yet another inquiry from the growing mass of critters in front of the classroom door.

"He brought them for us to kick and work out our stress on," came a reply.

"No I didn't," I retorted, "I brought them for me to kick and work out my stress, from having to deal with all you sophisticated intellectuals, egg-headed geniuses, midget sleuth detectives and . . . and if anyone even so much as thinks about touching one of these boxes, I'll throw myself from the roof of this building!"

"All right, grab a box everybody! Just don't allow yourself to think about it."

"Hooray, I want this one."

"Do you need help getting up on the roof? We'll help you, it's only one story high."

"He's fearless, our teacher."

"Isn't he great?"

"Yes, but his intellectual abilities leave something to be desired—but he is very kind."

There was exactly one box for each child and yes, the boxes were to help release some tension. Just how many ways can one use a box? I was soon to find out as 35 or so wonderful little monsters proceeded to kick their box, soccer style, across the football field.

Some kids completely destroyed their boxes, and such is what I mostly expected them to do. Others kept their box to play with or kick around later in the day. A few fondly (yes, fondly) brought their box into the class to either sit in, if it was large enough, or to put it to some other creative use.

I felt a tug at my sleeve as we went into the classroom and a little chipmunk of a face said to me, "I found something special to put into my box."

"What is that?" I asked.

"Me!" the chipmunk said, with a beaming smile of inspired delight.

"Yes," I said, "that is a very special thing to put into your box. Very special indeed."

What was so special about the chipmunk ? She didn't used to believe that she was special. Lately I had been seeing that self-awareness growing more and more and I had been nurturing it whenever possible.

What was so special for me? This was the first time she had voiced the fact that she was special. Now that's special.

Chapter 22
Lamps Are So Simple

There is ample and convincing research on the ill effects of traditional fluorescent lighting. I was aware of this fact, and I presented the school with the research and asked if they would consider switching to full-spectrum fluorescent lighting. It is more expensive for this natural lighting and the school must always consider the budget, so of course the lighting stayed the same.

Actually, that last statement is not implicitly true. Full-spectrum lighting is not more expensive, and only some of the lighting stayed the same. Full-spectrum lighting is only more expensive at first when compared to the traditional lighting that tends to disrupt the peaceful harmony of the human brain. I will not attempt to explain this phenomenon or to sell the product at this time. The information is out there and the reader can check it out for him or herself.

While the lighting stayed the same in the rest of the school, it changed in our classroom. The fluorescent overhead lights stayed off and were quickly replaced by table and floor lamps, much to the delight of the students. The atmosphere of the class, the room, and its occupants was noticeably more pleasant and at ease compared to other more standard classrooms. Visitors quickly noticed the difference, commented on it, and when their visit was over, left with somewhat of a special feeling inside.

In the long run the cost, if one were to only think in such terms, was less. To my way of thinking it could have cost twice or three times as much and it would have been far less expensive. If we do not strive for quality in what we do, how can we expect what we do to be or become quality? Where quality is concerned, every little bit counts. And most of those little bits are free for the taking. They need not cost at all and may well pay much in the long term.

Chapter 23
We Had A Bank—Sure

"We have a bank in our class," one of the secretaries was explaining to some visitors from a school district in a neighboring state. I was, again, dispossessed from my desk by the other secretary and was forced to sit on the couch with the end table, lamp, oval braided rug beneath my feet, and various pillows to lounge upon. And lounging indeed was what I was doing—thinking of a nap, in fact (hmm, could I pull it off in class?). I'd be willing to bet that if I were to doze off, the class would take pains to not disturb me and to fully respect my need for rest or contemplation. The only reason I didn't take advantage of this privilege was my paranoid fear of waking up bound and gagged while the class auctioned off my desk, chair and couch to the highest bidder.

I had just completed an intense discussion with the class regarding the death of a grandparent of one of our class members. The whole thing started with the child, whose grandparent died the day before, telling me that she would need extra hugs to help her get through the day. The first hug started the tears, and successive hugs from members of the class started more tears from others, who, at one time, had a member of their family pass away, or a pet run over, or a friend of a friend who lost a friend. One boy stated that he didn't know why he was crying other than, for some reason, it just felt good to do so.

About the time I began to wonder what the best move on my part was, the problem was taken in hand by the original bereaved girl. "I want to talk about this!" she said, in a rather angry (to my surprise) voice. "I am not only sad, I am angry about not having my grandma anymore."

It was a good group discussion that evolved from tears to good feeling and smiles. The class was now at work tying up loose ends on individual projects and such. I was lounging, in my think mode, digesting the last 45 minutes when our visitors arrived and were met by the welcoming committee. I was introduced, and the tour began.

"That's nice sweetheart, we have play banks in some of our classrooms, too. They're fun, aren't they?" was the visitor's comment to the secretary's statement of, "We have a bank in our class." I couldn't blame the visitor, because I always tend to cringe when I hear the term "classroom bank," as it gives me the image of playing bank or playing school.

"We have a banking system very much like the banks in town," said the secretary. "We all have money in the bank, checking and savings accounts, checks, deposit and withdrawal receipts and interest. We are working on a loan department to go into operation soon, but I'm afraid that may have mixed blessings. Do you know what I mean when I say 'mixed blessings'?"

The lady was standing there with her mouth open in awe (I hope) of the oratory skills of this somewhat precocious "mixed blessing" standing in front of her. I just sat there and watched. I wouldn't turn our girl Lucy (named after the Peanuts character) on my worst enemy. Lucy was just getting warmed up. The one thing she could not, would not, tolerate was a patronizing tone from an adult. This particular visitor just, innocently enough, made one strike against herself with the tone of her comment. "Sweetheart" was not one of Lucy's favorite terms of endearment. It just did not fit her personality. I could only hope that the woman did not—oh no; do not reach out and pat Lucy on the head, lady—too late. The damage was done. Strike three. No need for strike two even.

Lucy withstood the pat with amazing stoic acceptance. She had been working on self-control and doing quite well as of late. She hadn't sent one kid (or adult) to the nurse in over a month now. Maybe this will be the final exam for her graduation from some kind of little animal to some kind of little child, or midget adult, with a chip on her shoulder, disguised as a little child. At any rate, I was ready to stand up on the couch (a breach of proper class manners) and applaud Lucy's success at self-control and therefore subsequent graduation, or to throw the Australian boomerang, mounted on the wall behind me, that I kept for such emergencies as knocking out wild rabid wallabies or wild little midgets foaming at the mouth about to attack innocent visitors.

The pat on the head was, in itself, quite enough for strike three. The condescending smile that followed it was a runner up for strike four. If there was ever any doubt about the possibility of strike four being earned by our well-intentioned visitor, it was cinched by her comment to follow.

"Honey, I'll bet y'all are great little bankers."

The class, to my tuned ears, suddenly took on a quiet and ominous tone of cataclysmic expectation. Maybe it was the word "Honey" that pushed the awareness, even though everyone was diligently working away and minding (very intentionally at this point) their own business, over the brink of expecting to finish projects to expecting to call out the SWAT team momentarily.

Lucy smiled (this could mean danger or a determined effort at self-control). The lady smiled (but kept her hands to herself—maybe realizing that one pat was enough), the class waited in anticipation, thoughts of preparing rope, straight jacket and injection of tranquilizer dominant. I was already catatonic and visualizing yelling "recess" or "free ice cream" or some such desperate attempt at distraction while I ran outside and buried my head in a large anthill I knew to exist just three miles in the wilderness beyond the school property line.

Honey, I mean Lucy, calmly stated that she was not qualified to be a banker since she had not yet completed the four hours of on-the-job training at one of the banks in town. This was true. She had only two of the four completed and was very much intent on the other two next week. Being a banker was okay, but it was bank president she was after and she would settle for no less.

Honey—Lucy was presenting all this through a firm jaw and a non-wavering smile. Only I and the 35 members of the class caught the threat of danger underlying the determination in Lucy's voice. We breathed a sigh, in unison, that slightly fluttered the curtains around the windows and caused the front door latch to rattle as though someone opened and closed a door at the rear of the classroom.

The president of the bank relaxed enough to release his grip on the sides of his chair, stood up, and walked over to Lucy and the lady to introduce himself. "I'll be glad to explain the details of our banking system if you are interested," he said to the lady after the introduction.

"That won't be necessary," Lucy stated (a statement that left no room for discussion). "Unless of course, you, madam, prefer someone other than myself . . ." her voice trailed off at the ultimatum.

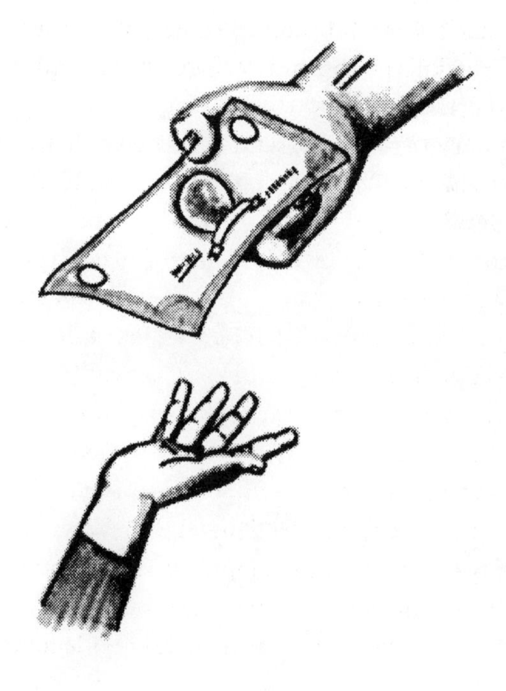

The tour was a success, Honey (I could hardly think of her as Lucy any longer) was a true success, and the last I remember was her giving the lady a big hug before she left with the other visitors.

"Honey," I said, "You were great." Her face took on a deadpan seriousness as she looked me straight in the eye and said, "I almost lost it when she called me that. I actually thought of grabbing her lower lip and simply falling to the floor." I almost gagged trying not to laugh at the visual impression. "How much weight can a lower lip hold, do you know?" she then asked. I sputtered my laughter into a choke and pretended to blow my nose into a tissue as tears of mirth tried to squeeze their way out of the corners of my eyes.

"Did I do well?" she asked.

"You did very well," I answered. "Your knowledge of the banking system is quite extensive—"

"That's not what I mean and you know it!" she said.

"Honey, your self-control was superb. I'm very proud of you. I think you are special."

That got me a beaming smile and a bear hug around the neck. "You know," she said, "She really was a nice lady. I hope she comes back soon."

"You're a secretary, send her an invitation."

"I will, I will."

Chapter 24

We Also Had A Class Store

Our class store was one of a kind. Perhaps it could only have existed in our class. I'm probably wrong. I hope so. I hope that many classrooms experience such a store, and better.

Money had to be earned with which to buy stock for the store, in order to have something for the store to sell to those who wanted to buy such goods. This concept was readily understood by the class. Of course, they would rather have simply had me use my own money to purchase the store inventory rather than think of ways to actually earn money themselves. But the earning of money was rather easily solved. If we could set up a kitchen to cook a turkey dinner we could certainly start a bakery for quality baked goods to sell to the other classes in the school.

With ingredients donated by parents, and baked items as well—for we could not produce enough fresh baked items from our one oven—we held a bake sale out of our front door once a week and raked in the bucks. These bucks purchased stock for our store from the big store downtown, such as wristwatches, small calculators, jewelry, pens, pencils, tablets, sports equipment and a wide range of popular toys (with the exclusions of war toys or toys that advocated violence). Our store also carried such novelty items as non-perishable gourmet foods: caviar, fried grasshoppers (a more popular item than one would think), olives, bamboo shoots, and various other Asian, European, Hungarian and Martian delights. Often a can of something would be purchased, opened, and never consumed, other than touching it to the tip of the tongue (if one could get it that close to the nose), whereupon the contents would be dissected and discarded.

"Boy, I'm glad I didn't buy a case of that stuff!"

Kids were able to encounter numerous new taste experiences (this kid as well), often not only to find that they had an affinity to a new item, but to find it also interesting to study and learn about a people and a culture that included such items in their everyday life. Not once did I ever suggest that such a study be done. There was enough stimulated curiosity to ensure that. Besides, they were ever on the alert for information with which to show my total lack of education, intelligence and wit. And the more bizarre the better.

The kids, of course, earned marks through various projects and work in class, and they all had marks to spend at the class store. It was especially delightful when a Christmas or birthday present was purchased by a child who would otherwise be unable to make such a (grand, in many instances) purchase. Whether the item was for oneself or another, it was worked for and earned in a most respectful way. They needed no one to tell them that.

It took a rather serious decision process to justify a purchase of an item from the store. There were many other things marks could purchase; some were basic living necessities.

First, there was the reality of rent or property payment for certain popular desk seating areas. Mechanics work area time could be purchased in addition to the normal, no-cost time, as well as various privileges, including free time to play outside. There was always the decision process confronting one when it came to spending marks. After all, marks in a savings account earned interest and "If one had enough savings, could one possibly live off the interest?" Such was a question put to me by one student.

"I think I have it figured out," he said. "I could earn enough to retire by the last quarter of the school year and only spend my interest."

"I would like to be able to do that," I said.

"I could actually buy enough free time where I wouldn't have to do any work at all during the last few weeks of school!" he stated with a far away look on his eyes.

"You would be bored to tears," came a comment from another student. "I've already thought of that one, and rejected it as stupid. Very stupid."

"Yeh, and if you wanted to do something in class you would probably have to pay because you would no longer be a working member—you'd be retired!"

"That's not a bad idea," I said, "I hadn't thought about charging you folks to come to school!" At that comment I rather expected panic and tearful pleading to persuade me not to charge them for the privilege of coming to school. What I actually received was something rather different. Soon it was me on bended knee in terrified pleading.

A small committee quickly approached me, with hands on hips and grin on lips, and stated: "We've been thinking about forming a board for hiring a new teacher."

"Yes, we feel that we could save some money by hiring a long term substitute . . ."

" . . . One who would be willing to let us play more softball."

"Play ball!" I yelled, and ran for the field in hopes to be first up to bat. That was a close call.

A handout I once received at an education workshop. It's worth sharing.

I Believe In You
I want to tell you that I believe in you.
I believe in your mind
And all the dreams, intelligence,
And determination within you.
You can accomplish anything.
You have so much open to you,
So please don't give up on what you want from life
Please don't put away the dreams inside of you.
You have the power to make them real.
You have the power to make yourself
Exactly what you want to be.
Exactly what you want to be.
Believe in yourself the way I do,
And nothing will be beyond your reach.

Chapter 25
A Real Creep

Have you ever met a kid who was a real creep? I have. Quite a few in fact. Whenever we had a kid who was a real Creep we took every opportunity to snub, reject, avoid and exclude the Creep. Everyone would ignore the Creep and he or she would get the message that they were different and not wanted. The Creep would suffer and we would all be indifferent to the suffering.

You had to pay in order to be the Creep. Sounds crazy, doesn't it? But it was true. The challenge was being a good Creep, even in the face of adversity, rejection, teasing and exclusion. The challenge was there, the opportunity was made available, and the Creep was expected to—but not really expected to be able to—do the work in class. Not everybody was up to taking on the life and trials of a Creep. But some did and paid cash (marks) on the barrel head (desk top) for the experience.

The Creep wore a burlap bag (itchy), with a hole that allowed only one arm to be free (limiting) and was snug around the legs below the knees (uncomfortable). The Creep was disfigured, handicapped, ugly, and didn't speak very well, if at all (by personal choice). The Creep was different. The Creep was not intentionally harassed or made fun of, just not accepted. One couldn't, or wouldn't, identify with or communicate with a Creep.

I served as a mentor, a safe place, but not a hiding place, for the Creep. Some kids who chose to play the Creep quit after only a few minutes of rejection or scorn by the others. The Creep would wander around or attempt to do class work. The problem was that no one really wanted to be near the Creep. Words of, "Go away, Creep," or "Get out, Creep," or "You smell," were heard regularly as the class went about its business. Disgusting looks and others staring or talking about you were par for the course of a Creep.

"They don't understand" I counseled, "some people are uncomfortable or even fear others who are different," I explained to the Creep. "It is only ignorance on their part . . ." "Try not to allow it to affect you . . ." "It's what is in your heart that counts . . ." and on and on. Some kids said that the rejection didn't bother them at all. But I wondered if rejection was so common in their non-Creep lives that there was no big difference for them as a Creep.

I was really careful with this "Creep" experience. It told me, and the class, a lot about ourselves as humans. We talked about our fears, weaknesses and defenses, our strengths, our differences and our many similarities.

We talked about things close to us and meaningful. We talked about our hopes, our beliefs and prejudices. We talked a lot. And as we talked, we understood more of ourselves. And as we better understood ourselves, we began to understand others. As we began to better understand others, we were more able to accept and to love. We talked a lot and it was good.

Chapter 26

The Day We Had A Hanging

The "Chipmunk" could hang. She was the undisputed champ in hanging and no one came close to out-hanging her.

A small group was engaged in a conversation about women in sports which was sparked by some research for a report a couple of students were preparing. The discussion group grew and began to get a little heated as a couple of the more athletic boys joined in. They were tauntingly making remarks about how boys were just naturally better athletes than girls, and the girls, as they joined in, taunted right back about boys only having larger muscles but not better brains or coordination, and so on.

I was dragged, literally, into the group as I began edging towards the door to see if maybe the principal had a little extra room under his desk for another person. The situation wasn't quite to the point of riot, but I could see it was likely to end up in either riot or civil war and I simply wanted to remain neutral. Hence the space under the principal's desk.

As I approached the lynch mob, I quickly expressed my enthusiasm to be of assistance. I said, "Don't look at me to solve this! I want no part of it."

The girls immediately retorted with, "We don't expect you to solve anything—after all, you're a boy!" and "Yeah, you'll probably just take sides with the boys!"

The boys hopped on the bandwagon with that, and said, "Yeah, tell the girls how much better boys are at sports!"

I had been prepared for this (knowing some of these boys as I did) and had my philosophical discourse all mentally prepared to expound upon the many historical female figures who have excelled in the world of sports. I cleared my throat and said, "Ah, well, I . . . a . . ."

"There have been many women, according to my research, that have excelled in the world of sports!" piped in one of the girls who was preparing the report that set this whole thing in motion.

"Ah . . . yes . . . just what I was going to . . ."

"That's right. They have even set world records," chimed in her partner in research.

"Oh yeah? You'll never convince me of no puny, weak female setting a world record," said one boy.

"I'll bet it wasn't in something important like basketball," said his buddy.

I could see that the boys were going to get some mileage out of this. They knew only too well that there were girls in the class that were better than they were in a number of athletic activities, but they had the girls' dander up and they were going to run with it all the way to the finish line. Well, both sides may learn something out of this. We had spoken before about people and causes, how far some people will defend something, to the point of becoming blind to right or wrong or anything moderate or gray. We had also talked about what fanaticism was. Now we'll see if anything was retained from those discussions.

"Basketball!" screamed one girl, "That's all you ever think of is basketball! You eat basketball cards for breakfast—of course, you are too illiterate to read them!" she continued.

She was hot! "Illiterate," that was good. But, of course everyone knew that this boy was anything but illiterate.

"You're right, I do eat basketball cards for breakfast. That's why I'm so smart!" he said with a smile and an expanded chest.

Another girl jumped in saying, "Smart?! If you had any brains you'd be dribbling them on the court during recess!"

It went on like this for a while, until I felt that everyone had the opportunity to express their best witticism, then I suggested that we have a hanging. Everyone seemed to be in favor of a hanging—but before they got too involved in the collective behavior of it all (that was another topic of discussion a short time past) and allowed the dynamics of the crowd (soon to possibly be "mob") sway them down a path of unknown hazards and thorns, they asked for my definition of a hanging.

Taking advantage of the captivated attention, I stressed a few concepts and made a few points, pertaining to the discussion at large, before explaining what a hanging was.

"It's simple," I said. "We all go out to the bars on the playground and see who can hang by their hands the longest."

The girls discovered that they could basically out-hang the boys—especially the stout and more husky boys. The "Chipmunk" could out-hang everyone. Hands down. No contest. She would just hang there with her chipmunk smile and those chipmunk cheeks, looking around and watching them drop one by one!

"I don't understand how she can do it," said a boy, shaking his head and flexing the pain out of his red palmed hands.

Another commented, "There's no end to her! She just hangs there and hangs there like there's nothing to it." He, too, was working his fingers and appeared a little surprised but relieved that they still worked.

The girls were grinning and saying nothing (there was some learning taking place here after all), and the boys were shaking their heads and rubbing their hands.

And the cute little Chipmunk would just hang, looking around and grinning her Chipmunk grin.

That was the day we had a hanging.

Chapter 27
Never Picked Last

I remember the kids who were always last to be picked for a team sport. I remember how they looked and how they felt. Sometimes it was I who was last or almost last to be picked. It caused me to feel terrible about myself and about those who wouldn't pick me. Under such circumstances, how could any person who was picked last do well in the game?

Friends picked friends even if they were not the best players. So if you were not picked until the end, that could tell you two—actually three—things: others didn't like you, you were not a good player, and that you really weren't worth much. Being picked last told you a lot of things that you believed were true because they were told and shown to you so often.

Even as a small child I used to think the process of "choosing" players was somehow cruel. I used to watch those chosen last die inside by little pieces at a time. I could see it take place right before my eyes; the degradation, the destruction, the death of another small piece of another small human being.

Sometimes, those who were picked last would try to compensate for their "lack" in other ways. Some acted out in class, some intentionally hurt or were cruel to others, some grew into bullies, others just held it in, turned it against their own selves.

We never chose teams. I simply said, "Okay, this group on one team and this group on the other team. Now who hasn't been captain in a while?" The kids knew; they didn't like the picking process either. We always cheered members of the other team, we encouraged those who tried no matter what their level of skill in the game. We almost always forgot to keep track of the score and we always, each and every one of us, had fun and felt good about ourselves and each other in the process.

"What's the score?"

"I don't know, I keep losing count."

"Me, too."

Chapter 28
Hoax

The Piltdown Man, the Perpetual Motion machine, an assortment of contraptions and gadgets, the society that claimed it was indecent for animals not to wear clothes and on and on and on—the study of hoaxes was a fascinating one indeed. Who's to say if maybe some of these wild ideas were simply a little ahead of their time and, in fact, with a change here or something added there, actually contributed to a real invention in time.

The interest in hoaxology was an intense one to say the least. The class was turned ablaze and wanted to invent a grand hoax to amaze the world; like the rumor that there would be a national shortage of toilet paper—but someone else had already thought of that. Then there were the college students who would drive up to Old Faithful in Yellowstone Park a few minutes before it was due to go off, whereupon they would make a production out of carrying a giant key off to the side of the tourist viewing area. With grand theatricals one student would hold a stop watch in his hand and at the proper moment signal the other students, who had already placed the key in a previously prepared receptacle, to turn the key and, to all appearances, start the flow of Old Faithful.

I told the kids of the hoax my dad played on his friends and on my mother many years ago. He claimed to be able to "feel" with his finger tips the suit of a playing card if it was a heart. He baffled everyone for a long time with that one. He never failed to be able to feel a heart on a playing card, if he was in the right mood. The right mood, a dining room table or a card table and me sitting across from him. I was his accomplice, the one who pressed my foot on his foot every time he held a card (facing away from him for all to see) that had a heart. Most everyone knew there was a gimmick to it; especially if they thought about it for a bit, but they just couldn't quite figure it out.

Like I said, the kids were anxious for a hoax. They had had their share of tricks and hoaxes from me, and this time they wanted to do it themselves. They had my blessings, and I told them that I hadn't been able to pull a fast one on them for a long time now. They were too sharp for me and therefore should try their hand at the art.

The only problem was to figure out a good hoax. The ground rules were already covered and quite familiar concepts to all. This was not to hurt or cheat anyone but simply to deceive, like sleight of hand in magic, and to entertain, like the special effects and advanced scientific concepts in Star Wars or Star Trek—Star Trek! That's it! Scientific concepts that are impossible today, improbable tomorrow, and matter-of-fact next week. It was the brainstorm of the year—of the century! And I had thought of it!

But I stopped in mid-flight and my face dropped as I said: "But forget it. It won't work."

"What?" they said. "What?"

"No, no. It won't work. Beam me up, Scotty, my phaser won't really work—nice idea though, and my communicator is too small to be real . . ."

"No, it's not!" someone said. "With microchip technology it is now possible!"

"What?" they said. "What? Tell us your idea."

"You are right," I said. "Dick Tracy's wrist radio actually came to be, and . . ."

"What?" they demanded. "What!?"

"Well," I said, looking down at the ground and shuffling my feet. "I thought, that you could—if you wanted to—"

"We want to, we want to. Tell us!"

"Only if you want to" (I couldn't play that out much longer). "You could enter hoax projects in the science fair, but," I rapidly blurted, "you said that you didn't want to participate in it this year so I didn't sign our class up and I don't know if it is too late for an entry at this time since the deadline for signing up is past and . . ."

"We want to do it! We must be able to get in—you can pull some strings can't you?"

"I can create a scientific experiment that will convince anyone that a particle beam can actually work."

"Yes. My project will be an explanation on light speed actually being too slow to allow real exploration in outer space."

"And I can help you with that. Have you ever heard of the idea that space may actually fold and that it may be possible to jump across it . . ."

"Good idea. I was actually thinking of FTL's, Faster Than Light ships but . . ."

"How about intelligent life on other star systems . . ."

"I would like to prove that space actually doesn't exist. If we are going to do hoax projects, we may as well do them right."

I sat back and watched and listened. The more I shrugged my shoulders, the more I showed some doubt about whether it would work or not, the more they got fired up. I was finally told that I must at once go to the office and pull some strings, threaten, bribe or cry in order to get our class accepted as an entry in the Science Fair.

I went to the bathroom, stopped by the teacher's lunch room and had a snack, checked my mail and, judging the time to be right, returned to class. A frenzy of ideas and concepts that appeared impossible but maybe were only improbable were being set to paper and pen in the hopes that they would appear believable.

I was hero of the day. I managed, barely, to get us in the Science Fair. I was also hero the day of the fair as we walked away with every award and honor to be had. Maybe it helped to be the only class in a new category, that was created just for us, but still and all, there were some very impressive and convincing displays. Not to mention the very convincing, "mad scientist-like" oral presentation by some of the class members.

The principal presented the awards: "It is my great pleasure to present the 'Overall Best Category' award of the Science Fair, to the category of Possible Improbabilities." He continued: "I was duly put to task by a couple of young scientists, who challenged me to prove that the world is indeed not flat. Their arguments were most convincing as were those of the scientists who have evidence that the world is actually hollow. I cannot dispute either proposal. After all, Admiral Byrd did testify to have flown inside the earth through a hole at the North Pole."

It's great to be a hero. I was basking in the beam of my inflated ego and thinking of the fast one I pulled on the kids, when the kid who was going to prove that space does not exist came over to me with a pin.

"You think you pulled a fast one on us, don't you?" he said, as he punctured my inflation with his pin.

"Why, what do you mean?" I asked, with pure innocence written all over me.

"I have this theory. Not a scientific one, but never the less, a theory . . ."

"Would you like some refreshment?" I asked. "Here, please, allow me to serve you some ice cream."

"Are you bribing me?" he asked, with a sly look in his eye.

"Yes, I am." I said. "And I will also flatter you with praise about your expansive genius and the fact that I have totally accepted your proposal regarding the need to reassess space."

"There is actually nothing to assess," he said.

"You have encouraged me to do some research of my own."

"Oh?" he commented.

"Yes, I'm going to prove that you do not exist. Starting with your name and grades in the book."

"Thank you," he said. "I am sure you will truly enjoy having me in your class next year."

He was smiling at me through his ice cream and I told him that I thought he would make a great teacher. He told me that he would like to teach science—but just a little differently from the standard approach. I have no doubt that he will do just that.

Chapter 29
This Newspaper Reporter Came To Interview Me

Reporter: Your class seems to be the talk of the town. Tell me, as a teacher, what is it that you do that makes this class so popular?

Me: As a classroom teacher I dabble in anxiety, high risk and mild forms of terror. All self-inflicted, of course. (Here I go again. Why can't I just do a normal interview like any other teacher would? Never mind—don't answer that.)

Reporter: Can you, uh, elaborate on that just a little?

Me: Personally, I think that the most wonderful experience is to stimulate the interest of a bunch of kids, to near manic excitement, over an almost unimaginable but possible improbability in investigative learning.

Reporter: An unimaginable possible improbability . . .

Me: <u>Almost</u> unimaginable. Then I love to sit back, in a mild state of anxiety and encroaching terror at the risk I just ventured upon, and watch them go about the process of, not only how to meet the challenge, but how to do me "one up" in the process.

Reporter: Do you "one up"?

Me: Right. Half the fun of it, for them, that is, is to better me with more than I asked—well, actually dared—them to do; even though I subtly implied that the problem was beyond their capabilities and level of intelligence . . .

Reporter: Dared them . . . You mean you actually implied that they would be unable to do it?

Me: Well, sort of, in a way I did. I told them that their brains were small, their growth was incomplete and that they should consider themselves fortunate that they were able to speak in sentences, but that in my superior intelligence and wisdom I was able to forgive them for their short comings. Pun intended. (His eyes began to glaze over. That's a good sign. He is about to make a shift in consciousness that will allow him to see things from a different perspective—a paradigm shift.)

Reporter: Uh, uh, you, you said that?

Me: Apparently they didn't believe me—ever since the time I misspelled the word "intelligence" on the board. It's sort of like stirring up a nest of bees. Killer bees, come to think of it. They don't easily let up and they certainly do not let you sit back for very long. It also seems like they usually come out on top of the whole thing.

Reporter: They, they actually come out on top? What do you mean?

Me: They love to try and make me out as some kind of incompetent bumbling fool who was awarded a teaching credential simply to quiet his incoherent babbling, or they attempt to redirect my interest in education to a more sedentary vocation like prison reform, or some harmless occupation like politics. They have even hinted at early retirement for me, and have recommended a good rest home with high walls and visiting privileges to school on weekends and holidays.

Reporter: You said that all in one breath.

Me: I didn't use any punctuation. You see, I'm a rather smug guy and I love to strut around in front of the class praising my larger brain and greater physical presence (all 145 pounds of it), saying, "I told you so."

Reporter: You do?

Me: Yes, I am looking forward to being able to do just that before the end of the school year.

Reporter: But the school year is almost over now!

Me: Oh, I'm usually able to lord it over them at least once a year. I save my best tricks for last—when I'm the most desperate. I must admit though, this group has been exceptionally tough this year. Last year's bunch were like that too. And the year before, come to think of it.

I only get one minute, you understand.

Reporter: One minute?

Me: I can only strut and say "I told you so," for one minute each time. Of course they have the same privilege, you know.

Student: Excuse me for interrupting, but I just wanted to, for the sake of accuracy in this interview, inform you that much of what he is telling you is probably an exaggeration of the truth and a stretching of the facts. He is really very nice to us and we all love him dearly.

Reporter: That came out of the mouth of a child?

Me: Yes, but she did use punctuation and took one breath. You know what they say, "Out of the mouth of babes," and all that.

Reporter: You look concerned.

Me: Worried is more like it. They're up to something, I can feel it.

Reporter: You can? They look like such nice kids.

Me: If you only knew. Inside each brain—as small as it may be—is a creative genius just waiting to be unleashed. And they're planning to use me as their victim to feast upon! Careful, you may be next.

Reporter: . . .

Me: Look at them. See the smug assurance about their presence? They are simply emanating that essence that tells me that they are confident in their ability to deprive me of my one minute!

Reporter: How, how can you tell?

Me: Do you hear it? The music? Not the Mozart Serenade in G that is playing on the stereo over there. But the other music, "The Twilight Zone."

Reporter: Yes. Yes, I do believe you are right! I hear it too. And, and, you know, I realize now that I've heard it before. "The Twilight Zone"—you know? Do-do, do-do . . .

Me: You hear it too? (A major breakthrough—he's going to make it yet.)

Reporter: You're right about the kids. I think I can sense a little of what you are saying. I mean, it seems to me that they believe they are going to, to . . . Well, to be frank with you, I don't think you are going to get your minute in front of the class this year. Sorry.

Me: Speaking of high anxiety, risk and terror, wouldn't you like to interview some of the small people in the class? Lucy is out at the moment, intimidating some eighth grade students in a debating contest. But she'll be back before you leave. She's making some rather impressive advancements in channeling her unique abilities into more constructive outlets. Just call her Honey. She's doing quite well with that term of endearment.

Allow me to introduce you to my head secretary. He has rabies, but being a pacifist by nature he refuses to bite.

Before you leave the security of this couch behind my desk, it is necessary that I caution you about . . .

Reporter: I know, expect the unexpected. I'm looking forward to this experience.

Me: (Hmm. This guy learns almost as fast as some of the kids in here.)

Chapter 30
Mechanics Workshop

Children are curious and have a passion for probing into things. They like to see how things work and, if given an opportunity, love to take things apart. Once a kid gets into the swing of taking things apart, gets a feel for what tools and determination (with a little bit of ingenuity) can accomplish, a manic-like fever may take hold and transform the child into a "disassemblage" threat to anything that doesn't move. I was such a child.

My grandfather collected odds and ends to tinker with during his walks through the alley behind his house or on his way to and from town. My grandmother collected, from his collection, fascinating goodies for me to tinker with. Clocks and old radios were my favorites. Old alarm clocks offered a multitude of gears to be used as spinning tops, and radios provided wonderful electrical parts to be investigated. I even took apart the vacuum tubes! As I caught the "disassemblage fever" my motto at first came to be, "If it doesn't move, take it apart." As the fever grew my philosophy expanded: "If it moves, chase it down and then take it apart!"

I managed to get a lot of mileage out of my "disassemblage fever," and I hung on to that part of my childhood as long as I could. At the ripe old age of 16 I took apart my car when it quit running. Rather than fix it—well, I started out to "fix" it, but I became so fascinated by how things came apart and what was inside them that I just lost control and disassembled it! It was great fun.

Our classroom had a mechanics workshop. It was large enough to accommodate about six to eight kid mechanics at one time. The privilege of using the assortment of tools with which to take apart the wealth of interesting and fascinating things in the shop was available to all members of the class. Of course a tool safety lesson must be absorbed, understood and practiced, all electric cords must be cut off before disassembly begins and one must be up-to-date on his or her classwork. With those requirements fulfilled, one could indulge in the art of "mechanic's fix-it." Actually, nothing ever got fixed, just investigated and methodically disassembled down to its least common denominator, nut, bolt or screw.

Children seemed to enter a world of their own when working in the shop: Wonderful delirium, fever of the mechanical sort. Reality fades away taking all cares and woes. The brow is damp, the mind knows only the challenge of removal, disconnect, and separate as one discovers new, strange, and different forms. And via the parts, the pieces, the apartness, one somehow feels whole, confident and at peace within oneself.

Thrift stores, garage sales, wrecking yards and parents were our sources of clocks, toasters, radios, mixers, electric motors, typewriters, carburetors, generators, and anything that failed to tick, whir, or move. Kids became feverish with take-it-apart attacks. I had to watch them because if something stayed in one place too long or didn't seem to breathe or have some kind of pulse, they tended to reach for the tools. I monitored carefully what they brought from home: a stereo? Hmm, where did you get it from?? Not your older brother's room, I hope . . . Is that an antique . . . ?

Actually, such apprehensions were merely projections on my part, for I cannot remember anyone ever bringing anything to class but junk to be "fixed." What went on at home with their own tools, I refused to think about. And I've always wondered what happened to the insides of the large clock on the wall of the room. One day it simply stopped working, and when I climbed up on top of a desk to look inside, it was empty! Why would the school install a clock on the wall with no inside works? And how did it, at one time, appear to keep time when it was in fact empty? A mystery I may never solve. In fact, I'm not even really sure that it ever did actually run—a number of kids swear that it never did.

Humor

Humor is probably one of the best teaching/learning tools ever invented. Laughing with another is a great way to encourage friendship and to create a bond of togetherness. Laughter helps stimulate a feeling of cooperation. Laughter helps people like each other.

We always laugh *with* and never at another. One may (and must) laugh *at* oneself; others may join in and laugh *with* that person who is laughing at his or her self.

Laughing at self or laughing with another helps us to recognize the humor in our attempts at life and to not take our "lack of perfection" or accomplishments too seriously. After all, life is only practice, otherwise there would be no need for learning at all.

Chapter 31

I Feared For My Car In The Parking Lot

The abilities and skills of my miniature mechanics began to impress me more and more as time went on. They possessed, as all kids are quite capable of, an ability to persevere that can stagger the imagination of an adult. I suspect that many items were "worried," or "pestered" apart by sheer determination as much as they were by actual use of tools. I know for a fact that cars respond by the mechanic talking to them. I learned as a young mechanic, that certain words, phrases, and tone of voice can convince a stuck bolt on an engine to come loose. As any proper shade tree mechanic has learned, it just takes the right combination of words, voice emphasis, foaming at the mouth, etc. to fix a car.

The midget mechanics were much too young for such advanced concepts of mechanical psychology; at their age they simply muttered under their breath a little and created new and innovative ways to use tools in order to accomplish their purpose.

I had to watch "innovative tool use" rather closely. In the outside world new tools were designed and invented on a regular basis, and probably made the inventor famous and wealthy. Not wanting to discourage invention and creativity (and possible wealth and fame), I did not discourage experimentation. I only needed to be aware of it so I could view the safety factor and be a famous and wealthy witness of the inventive moment.

Soon the emerging mechanical skills, the determination, and the success rate to disassemble began to cause me growing concern. I began to carefully guard my watch as I caught coveting and covert glances at it from some of the more avid "mechanics." They were not looking for the time. I kept an eye on my personal calculator and the pencil sharpener on the wall. I regularly glanced at the lamps softly glowing in various places around the room—was there one missing? I tried to remember. I had a major concern on my mind, I must admit. I trembled in fear for my car, so near by in the parking lot.

I used to fantasize about how long it would take for a herd of experienced and frenzy-eyed dismantler gremlins, with tools in hand, to dissolve a classic Mustang into a scattered pile of itty-bitty classic pieces. I could imagine the ad I might run in the paper under classic cars: Parting out 1965 Mustang fastback. Small pieces only. Reasonable.

As much out of curiosity as an attempt to spare my Mustang, I came upon the grand idea of getting a junk yard vehicle for the kids to take apart. The thought came to me suddenly one day when a committee of gremlin mechanical fanatics approached me and said, "May we take your car apart?" I love the honesty of children. They did not ask if they "could" take my car apart; they knew very well that they were quite capable of reducing it to itty-bitty classic pieces. They were simply asking permission to do so. Like I said, I love the honesty of children. What I despise is their unmitigated, brazen nerve to dare ask me such a stupid question. Of all the unashamed nerve—the gall . . . I said yes. I gave them my permission. I agreed. I was also very preoccupied at the time.

Everyone in the class knew the art of polite interruption. Without such a skill, people would get upset with you for being rude when you butt into their conversation or concentration. In our class, without such a skill, you would never get a word in or ever be noticed as someone actually alive and breathing. Some people in our class actually honed their skill of interruption/interjection/interception into a fine but subversive art of criminal capability. These same demented minds took advantage of my intense preoccupation to stealthily time their question solely for their own gain and advantage. I could not help but envy their skill. Their timing was perfect. I had just removed my pay check from its envelope and was trying to understand why so much of it went to deductions.

"Yeah, sure, go ahead . . . as long as you are caught up with your work . . . mumble, mumble." What caught my attention was that the general sound level of the class lowered by just a fraction of a decibel. My eyeballs were involuntarily programmed, by years of experience with subversive, sneaky and sly mentalities—mainly my own as a young student in the educational system—so that the almost imperceptible audio change caused them, as if pulled by a marionette's string, to look up. The first thought of any good teacher is for the safety and welfare of the students. My first thought was—they're up to no good.

"What!" I said, as my eyes checked the lamps in the class, the door knobs, and I automatically felt for my wristwatch. "What?"

"See, he never listens to us."

"Yeah, we're not important."

"We could all stay home and he wouldn't even know it."

"Yeah, I'm going to stay home tomorrow and see if he notices."

"Me, too."

"All of us will. The whole class."

They didn't fool me one bit. Tomorrow was Saturday. Or was it? It couldn't be Saturday today, could it?

"What are you up to, gremlins?" I said as I put away my paycheck—can't believe how much is taken out each month . . .

"We're going out to the parking lot with the tools to take apart that funny little car you insist on driving. You gave us permission."

"I gave you permission?" I said.

"Yes, just a minute ago."

"Yes, very generous of you, actually."

"Indeed, he's really not a bad sort after all."

"Was that your paycheck you were looking at?"

"Didn't you once tell us that you didn't get paid for teaching?"

"I think he meant something different when he said that."

"Yes, like it was meant to go over our heads?"

"Right. It's called adult humor and kids aren't suppose to get it."

"Gremlins!" I said, "you are evading the issue. I did not give you permission to . . ."

"He's reneging—I knew it was too good to be true."

"Yes. He told a lie."

"Lie is not a very polite term to accuse someone of. "Prevaricate" is a word we were taught. Remember?"

"Yes. He prevaricated. And lied."

Although I had refused to give them extra credit outright for their ability to increase their vocabulary, I did suggest that such display of skillful oratory could very well sway, influence, even bribe me to give consideration to the higher grade over a lower one whenever such a decision was in the balance. I was living to regret such rash decisions. But their vocabulary did sound pretty good.

I could see I was going to have to take a firm stand. It was time to take control, so I said, "Alright, if you promise not to disassemble my car, I'll see what I can do about getting a junker for you to investigate. But no guarantee."

"We don't want to 'investigate' a car. We want to take it apart! In itsy, bitsy, tiny pieces."

At that point a black-eyed, raven-hair beauty came up to me and said, "You *are* aware that my *Daddy* owns a wrecking yard, aren't you?" she asked. This was true. A big one at that. There was an emphasis on the word "daddy."

"I'm sure that *Daddy* will be happy to donate one of his old broken cars to our class. I'll work on *Daddy* tonight. He finds it difficult to refuse me anything." I felt the poor man didn't stand a chance; as she stood there rubbing her hands together and giving me her most convincing grin, with plenty of teeth in it.

We were offered the car. Delivered. Any make or model, placed safely on the ground anywhere we would like it and removed, the pieces, whenever we wished.

The new principal would not allow it. He wouldn't even take me seriously. I was going to have to work on him. Maybe I'll set the raven-haired one on him, teeth and all. Meanwhile, his car was in the parking lot. It would be a lot more fun to take apart than mine—more pieces to it. Itsy bitsy, teeny weeny pieces. I could casually drop the hint that there may even be some extra credit in it. Extra credit for not getting caught while making itsy bitsy pieces out of a late model Cadillac. Now, wouldn't that be classic?

Chapter 32
A Hard Act To Follow

Open house is a time for teachers and students to show off their stuff. It is a time to impress parents with displays of projects and a classroom all decked out. But open house presented a problem for our class.

The problem was that our class was *always* decked out—with real decks, docks and other high-rise platforms and such. What more could we do? We always had projects on display because there was always some class project or a multitude of individual or small group projects going on. What else could we do? We were constantly showing off our stuff and impressing parents because we were usually doing neat and interesting stuff. Parents were in a constant state of "impressment" because we always included them in what we were doing. They didn't actually have much choice but to be kept up-to-date on the class activities when their child was fanatically involved, maniacally interested, and radically vocal about it. Our parents missed out on very little of what was going on. What could we do for open house? What else was there?

Once, a newly hired teacher made the comment to me, "You're a hard act to follow." The poor guy didn't know what to do in his class that would compare to what we were doing in ours. And now we found our own act hard to follow. We kept asking ourselves, what do we do for open house?

It was like asking what do we do for Halloween when everyday was trick or treat. Well, we solved it at last. All of us vampires, werewolves, monsters and gremlins would dress up as normal human beings. Well, almost. We simply decided to produce a video documentary. A production that would be a copy of a real

TV documentary with narrator, interviews, and a host to introduce it. It would be about our class. This was going to be a big project. I knew how big something like this could be because some years earlier I had written and directed a documentary for TV. I had spent a long time doing the research, and my partner, the producer, and I had spent months with storyboards, editing, filming, and meetings at the local TV station. The night it was broadcast on TV was, for me, the culmination of two years of work flashed across the screen in 20 minutes. It was a great film and I felt proud, but in my mind I had already begun improvements and revisions for the next version that was soon to be used in various universities across the nation for teacher education training.

The research for the class film was already done. The kids knew well how the class had evolved, all the projects, etc., etc. They knew their topic from, literally, the inside out. I served as consultant for production techniques and they created, wrote, directed, and produced a masterpiece documentary complete with host, introduction, narration and interviews all done within the time frame of two months. The little devils just had to do me one better. I was forced to admit that their two-month production was indeed more interesting, original, creative, and just plain better than my two-year one. It was also pointed out to me that their production, like mine, was also shown on TV. True, it was only one TV, one that belonged to the school, but it *was* shown on TV. From the reception given the documentary by parents, I had to admit total defeat. But revenge was to be mine and the means to come, unwittingly, from a parent.

Now, normally I am not a vengeful person. This was not normally. It was 35 against one, not to count the parents, siblings and other relatives. I decided to be a vengeful person, and enjoy it. At the end of open house, the last parents to leave paused as they were headed for the door. The woman said to me, "Is that another way to spell physical?" She was referring to the spelling, "phisical," on a number of posters, on one of the walls, showing the importance of balance in the sides of the mental, physical and emotional triangle of life. Rather than accuse me, as a teacher, of a misspelling, she assumed, as probably so many others had that evening, that there must be an alternate spelling of the word. She just had to solve the mystery of it. I'm glad she did, for now I had my revenge. I had them because no one caught it. Oh sweet one-upmanship. I couldn't wait for tomorrow to rub it in.

When this wonderful person pointed out my means of "payback," I was astounded that it ever got by me or the whiz kids who loved to catch me writing misspelled words on the board. That was another monster I created that served to regularly turn on me and bite at my heels. I freely admitted that I, an adult, teacher, emperor of the class, etc., was in fact a horrible speller, and if they were to catch me misspelling words, they were welcome to correct me with the proper spelling. I, in turn, would remember these corrections and allow myself to be coaxed into granting minor bits of gratuity at various times when a particular student found him or herself in need of a little extra leverage. The result was that as I wrote on the chalkboard, at any given moment pages of a dictionary could be heard whizzing in a flurry to correct my mistake—thus the name "whiz kids."

Dictionaries were kept at hand like six-guns, for the time when a quick draw was necessary. I used to misspell words intentionally on a hot day just to start the cooling breeze that a mass whizzing of pages would create. I would feverishly write treatises on science, psychology, anthropology, philosophy, wisdom (always a good one to stimulate a raging debate) and complicated dribble or directions that bordered on the fringes of impossibility or madness, with the occasional misspelled word.

It was early the next morning and I was smugly sitting at my desk, waiting to say, ". . . And nobody caught it during all this time," when a student came up to me and said, " You misspelled physical on the board a few days ago and everybody copied it on their posters that way." And I said, "And nobody caught it during all this time—but you."

"I'm one smart fella, aren't I," he said.

"You sure are. I think you deserve a big hug, too."

Hugs to this kid were the greatest treat in the world. For both of us, actually. To heck with revenge.

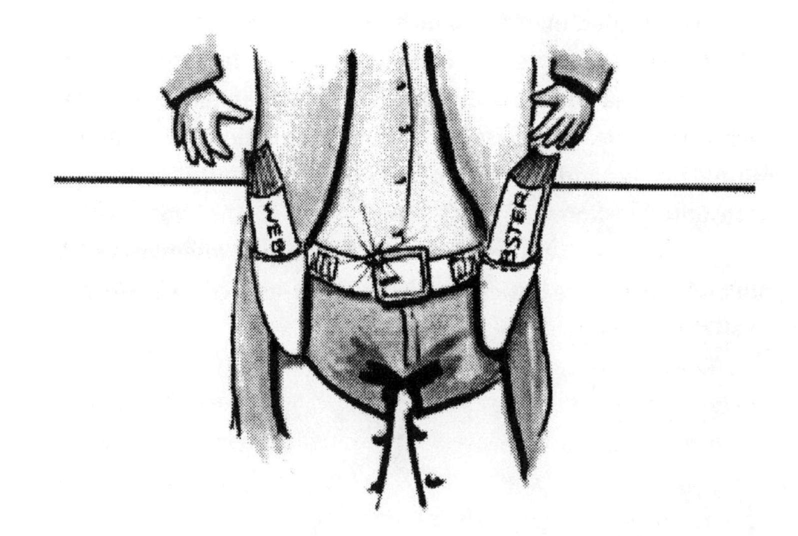

Our Class

Our class was not a "free" or "open" or "unstructured" (or whatever) class. I was following no model or system other than our (the kids' and my) invent-it-as-you-grow system. We did what was needed in order to meet our learning needs.

I don't even know if one can call our class democratic—maybe because I'm not really sure just what that may be or even if such is possible. Our class was simply a situation that expressed mutual respect and caring, fun and how much could we learn, do, share and question.

Our success was measured in how much love was felt for self and others. The basics, that is, the core subjects, were easy.

Chapter 33
A Very Special Privilege

Few teachers have the most delightful privilege of having their own child as a student in their class, although I have spoken to teachers that have described this "privilege" as not so delightful. Of course, I have also spoken to teachers who describe the experience of teaching school as less than delightful. Too bad, they should have had the class help them.

The experience of having my youngest son in my class was, for me, a real highlight. It was good for him but I'm sure it was better for me. In the class I was at my best. First of all, I was well trained and experienced before I became a full-fledged teacher with the responsibility of kids "all my own." Not so as a father. Like so many parents I was untrained, inexperienced, young and dumb. So I made a lot of poor decisions as a young father, and as an older father too.

I was better as a teacher than I was as a father and I knew it. As much as it hurt to admit it, admit it I must. So as a teacher I could offer my son more than I would ever have been able to if I never had the privilege to be his teacher. As a teacher I was able to see the trees; as a father I was too close to the forest. As a teacher I was able to stand back in order to be able to act more appropriately. I was to learn a lot about myself that year that would help me become a better person, a better teacher and, someday, a better parent.

I was always amazed when a teacher or a parent would say that they couldn't stand to have their child in their class or that they wouldn't want the experience. It took little effort on my part to treat my son equal to any other person in the class. I knew how important that would be and I explained it to him. He could understand because he was an intelligent person and had always, even as a baby, been a really fine individual. But it took a little shock for him to really realize that I meant what I said.

My son had always been popular. He was always fun and comfortable to be around. His popularity increased when he became part of the class and that, I believe, served to be a distraction for him—but only until first quarter report card time. He had always been a top student, by his own decision with no pressure from home. He was especially sharp in math and science (which I do not believe came from my side of the family) and it is ironic that math, his easiest subject, would serve to be his best teacher.

As much as he was reminded by me (yes, I admit this may be considered as a little extra fatherly attention), he failed to complete or turn in enough math assignments to earn a good grade. That presented a difficult decision for me. I could order him to do his missing math assignments (like a father), and he would have done them. They would have been done for me, for the grade and for all the wrong reasons. As a teacher I wanted him to do them for his own self. An "A" on a paper says the problems were completed and correct. There is no mark, other than written or verbal comments by the teacher, that says, "Congratulations, you did this for yourself and not because you were ordered to." I had no choice but to give my child a "D" in math. Among all those "A"s it stood out like a sore thumb and I cringed at the sight of it. But I knew it would serve a most valuable purpose. I hoped.

His face dropped when he saw it. Be strong, I said to myself. "I got a 'D' in math?" he said. By his surprise I knew that he either didn't "hear" my reminders, or he thought that Dad the Teacher would give him a good grade.

"I didn't have any choice," I told him. We both knew he could do the work. We both knew that he chose not to. We both also knew that the grade book was always there for students to see what work they were missing, and we both knew that there was plenty of opportunity to get the work in. No excuses, but it still hurt.

The problem was never to appear again and I feel that it actually helped him to feel more at ease. He could be a kid in a class and just do and be what a kid in a class would do and be. No pressure of the concern that Dad was the teacher. It was a very special privilege to have this child as a student in the class.

Chapter 34
Think Tank

"Think. That's all, just think. Think of it as a new and challenging experience. You may even grow to like it," I said, as the members of the class quizzed me about a proposed think tank as part of the class experience. The topic of think tanks came about from a research project drawn out of the Project Box of a "thousand and one" topics.

I continued, "Not only do you not have to do any class work during the time you opt to be part of the think tank team, but one of the rules is that you may *not* do any work. Just sit there, or pace around, and think. Come up with ideas." This must be a new concept in education. Even to me the idea of not allowing any work to be done was somewhat revolutionary. I know many students throughout the nation did their best to do just that, myself included as a young captive of the education confinement laws, but for a teacher to request such must be a first.

"You mean to tell us that we are not allowed to do work, just think?"

"Yes."

"Think of ideas?"

"Yes."

"What kind of ideas?"

"That's up to the thinker."

"Like ideas concerning the class?"

"If that's what the thinker thinks, yes."

"Ideas about playing? Sleeping? Walking? Food? Brushing teeth? World affairs? Crime? Inventions? . . ."

"You're hot. Ideas about anything you can think about. Just be sure to record everything."

"I could think about jokes."

"Yes."

"I'd like to think about thinking."

"Excellent."

"Really? You're serious? Just think about thinking?"

"Indeed. Consider the process of thinking. Quite profound when you think about it."

"And to think about the process of thinking about thinking!"

"You guys are hot. Really hot. So give this think tank concept some thought and let me know what you think of it. You can do it, if you're of a mind," They missed none of this play on words.

"Do we need to be caught up with our work in order to be part of the think tank project?"

"What do you think?"

"That's what we thought."

"See, we are already beginning to think!"

"Yes," thought I.

Thinking takes energy. It burns calories. It is work. It is said that if one can hold the attention, unwavering and focused, for even one minute, on an idea, concept, problem or goal, wonders may be achieved. It is estimated that our internal self-talk or mind talk (I call that rambling voice "Babbler") goes on at the rate of 1200 words per minute. That's pretty high-speed babbling! Focus these thoughts, control them, train them upon a goal, a dream or a solution and one begins to experience mastery of self. One begins to take control of one's life.

One begins to create, to invent, to be responsible for self. One begins to become more complete. Although one may have doubts about the actuality of this happening in our think tank when such thoughts of questionable wisdom as the following one occurs. But, if one really thinks on it—it may not be such a bad idea . . .

Think Tank Thought 074.65

Item: Business Venture
Lawn weeding and fertilizing business
Need: Enclosed truck, van or trailer
50 to 100 ducks (hungry)
Fact: Ducks like to eat weeds.
Method: Transport duck to customers lawn. Release hungry ducks on customers lawn for weed removal and fertilizing (duck).
Kinks to work out:
a) how to get ducks back in truck, trailer or van
b) how to get rid of flies that will be attracted by the fertilizer
Fact: Frogs eat flies.
My comments:
Excellent idea! If for some strange and unforeseen reason this enterprise should fail to live up to your expectations—well, it could be duck soup. I would like to offer my lawn for the testing of this project, but the weeds in my lawn are of such massive size as to actually be known to attack cats, chickens, kids and ducks alike. Question: Do alligators eat frogs?

On the whole, our think tank was productive, enlightening, and did produce, well, many concepts, ideas and thoughts to give us all something to think about for a long, long time. It also stimulated some brainstorming sessions the likes of which I have never experienced before or ever after.

Chapter 35
The End Of School

All good things come to an end. Of course, the end of one good thing is but the beginning of another good or even better thing.

The end of school had come for me. Something else was pulling me in its direction. At the time I wasn't sure what direction I was being pulled towards. I only knew that I had to follow a path that I had of late placed my foot upon. It was no path in particular other than that a quest had begun within me for greater understanding of my world, my place in it, and that which I called me.

Suddenly the school was too confining for me. I had learned, I had grown and I was about to graduate and go on to more learning and growing—just like one of the kids. I had had many good teachers (small, but good) and I felt humbled by what many of them could teach me yet.

But I had to go on. I did go on—I actually drove off into the sunset—and as I drove away it felt good inside. I was a little scared, I had no particular place to go, but I felt good about my decision. As it turned out my decision was good; in fact it was very good.

Gremlins, I'll miss you and I'll always remember you. We'll all remember the special times we had together: the laughter, the tears, the challenge, the fun, and always the love and caring that was shown towards one another; for therein lies the key to your success: the key to the success of humankind—if only they could learn and practice it so well as you have. I pray that above all, you have learned the importance of caring and showing that you care.

For myself, I plan to go live in the forest for awhile and begin a new life. I want to listen to trees grow, build a cabin, talk to deer, and disassemble my wristwatch in a meadow on a sunny fall day. Sounds off-the-wall, doesn't it? But I remember something a teacher of mine once said: "Dreams are important, don't you think so?"

I answered, "Yes, I do believe so; with all my heart."

This person went on to say, "I have decided to be a dreamer when I grow up."

"Me, too," I said.

"You mean you haven't grown up yet?"

"I'm working on it."

As I drove off into the sunset, I had to smile.

Child's Play
A microsociety in a variety of ways,
A drama of ourselves it is true.
As we witness the acts,
Do we see where we're at.
Through our little ones,
Do we see what we do.

Epilogue

On the first day of school I would say to the class:

"We are going to have the best class in the school. You are going to do more fun things than ever before in your life. We are going to learn a lot in this class, and much of what you will learn will be so interesting, so fascinating, and so enjoyable that you are going to want to keep on learning for the rest of your life! You'll never want to stop learning because, as you are about to find out, it's fun."

[First I set the scene, the game plan, the expectations, the suggestions that will be our definition of education.]

"But, it all depends on you. This is not just my class. It is your class—our class. And together with your help, with each one of us working together, this is going to be the best class ever. We'll be doing a lot of work in this class—a lot. We'll be doing more things in here than you ever thought possible. You are also going to have more fun than you ever thought possible."

[Then I begin to show where the responsibility for success will lie while reinforcing that such will also be fun.]

"I will do everything in my power to make what we do and study interesting, enjoyable, and amazing. In fact, some of what we will do and study in here is going to absolutely amaze you beyond belief. You'll be speechless. Guaranteed. You are going to be amazed, thrilled, scared, and fascinated by what you are about to learn and experience in this class. You will be happy, sad, outraged and delighted by some of the things you will learn in here. Some of you may cry because of what you learn. And, you're going to laugh. You are going to laugh until the tears squeeze out of your eyes."

[I give my commitment to offer them worthy experiences in education and let them know that it's not only okay to express their emotions, but that such will be accepted as part of the normal fare.]

"But—*[long pause]* this can only happen if I have your help and cooperation. It can only happen if each and every person in this class shows cooperation and respect for each and every other member of the class. It can't be done without that. We are going to be a big wonderful family. We're going to help and look out for each other. Each one of you is going to have a lot of others on your side."

[At this time of the year, I was considered to be some sort of minor demi-god, magician, or whatever. I fostered the reputation of being able to "pull rabbits out of hats," and did nothing to play down the mystique of my success with "poor" students or "incorrigible" children. To some, all that mattered was that our test scores always tried to go off the top of the charts each year, while we seemed to be having a good time, and only once in a while expressing a little strange behavior. Little did they know that the teacher came from a long line of vaudeville acts, and that he was simply up there "breaking a leg" and passing on the craft.

Now was the time to begin (least it go to my head) to place some of the "power," where it should be, with the kids. Remember, with power comes responsibility.]

"I only ask one thing of you, that you be self-responsible. Being self-responsible means being responsible for your decisions and actions. Simple as that. Easy. You all, each and every one of you, are able to do that. No problem."

[Talk about over-simplification! How many of us big kids can boast such self-responsibility?]

"If you can show that you are a self-responsible person, I promise that I will do everything in my power to see that you have every privilege possible in this school."

[Pause, to let that sink in.]

"In fact, (pause again) if you show that you are self-responsible—in control of your actions and decisions—I will *invent* extra privileges for you to have!"

[Self-responsibility was a term everyone would come to thoroughly know and understand during the school year. The concept could be

discussed at length. Responsibility carried over into the home. It was something that was accountable to self, by self and for self.]

"Now, I don't know anything about you. Some of you I have met on the playground from time to time last year, but I really don't know anything about you. I have not read your files in the office—I only skimmed through them looking for red tags of medical alert. I haven't seen any of your past report cards or talked to any of your past teachers. As far as I know you could all be 'A' students. In fact, I suspect, from what you have shown me so far, that you all are. All you have to do is act like a top student and you will fool me."

[Here I plant the seed that they all begin with a clean slate. I refused to chat with other teachers about the kids that were going to be in my class. I wanted that child to start fresh with me and to build his or her reputation from "here and now," not "there and then." This was a new game and we were all different players from what we were last year.]

"If you haven't been an 'A' student before now, don't worry. You will not be competing against any other person in this class. You will only be competing with yourself. That means that if you are responsible, use your time wisely and show that you are improving you will be getting top grades before you know it. Guaranteed. Even if you have never received an 'A' ever before, you will earn 'A's in this class."

[Each year as I said this to the class, I thought to myself how important it was to provide the experience for each child to succeed beyond his or her expectations, and to realize that there is a genius within. In everyone there is something special that can easily earn an 'A' or an 'A-plus' or even a double 'A'!

I thought of my own grade school experience as a student, of low and failing grades and of finally dropping out of school because I was bored to tears. None of it seemed to make sense or have relevance to my life and needs. I was not about to allow that to happen here.]

"Since this is your class and you are responsible for the success of it, you should, and will be, making decisions about how it is run. Don't you agree? I feel that is only right that you, as responsible members of the class, be able to make important decisions about what you will study and how you will learn. We all learn in different ways because we are all different, special and unique individuals. So it is only fair that you should have a say in the way that is best for you to learn. We'll talk more about what different learning styles are all about, so that you'll understand and be more able to make the right choices for yourself. I think that you will find that you are actually smarter than you think."

[I'm placing a lot of responsibility here on a lot of little shoulders, but I am also strengthening those shoulders with some empowerment and the hint that they just may be a little more capable than they have given themselves credit for.]

"If you have gotten poor grades in the past, you are going to suddenly find yourself earning much better grades here, because I am going to tell you some wonderful secrets on how to learn faster, easier and better than you ever have before. In fact, you're going to learn some things a lot of adults don't even know."

[More empowerment. Initiation into the secret world of knowledge and adults. The mysteries of learning revealed! They are soon to find out that adults (and teachers) do not have all the answers and are simply mortals like themselves. This is some heavy stuff.]

"We are going to talk about a lot of things during this next year. The reason we are going to talk is so we can all understand things. Because, how can you make a good decision, the right choice, unless you are able to understand the problem or what something is all about? So we'll talk about it. It is only fair to you. If you have a problem about something or if you feel a thing isn't right or needs to be changed, you have the right to be heard. You may talk to me about it alone, with a group of kids or the whole class. There is no problem we can't make better when we discuss it like the intelligent and caring human beings that we all are."

[The assumption is made that we are all intelligent and caring human beings—and so it is.]

The first quarter of the semester I talked to them a lot. It seemed like over half of our time in class was spent in discussion, with me doing, at first, most of the talking. I believe that if someone hears something repeated enough times and in enough ways, they will begin to believe it. I wanted them to believe in themselves. I wanted them to believe they were worthy and deserving of success—for many of them had had that feeling taken from or denied them. I wanted them to believe that they were top students, smart, sharp, deserving of love and worthy of all good things. I wanted to convince them that they could do just about anything they put their minds to.

By the second quarter we were spending less than half our time in discussion, and they were doing most of the talking. They wanted to convince me that they were top students, sharp and worthy of more than they thought I would allow them to do. They felt safe with me and secure in my love for them. This gave them self-confidence and a willingness to take risks, to seek adventure and be daring. They knew that they had a shelter if ever needed.

They wanted to convince me that they could do most anything they put their minds to. The amount of quality work being produced was becoming quite impressive.

Half-way through the semester found us still having discussions. Communication and ideas had become the core of our existence. The discussions had broadened out into multifaceted meetings that would create awe in the breast of state senators, philosophers, and university professors alike. The students no longer tried to convince me or themselves what they were able to do. They knew that there were few, if any, limits on their abilities or creativity.

My position, more and more, became one of facilitator. I would guide them into new directions and areas; I would hint and suggest and, more often than not, there would be the subtle challenge to push on the present limits. I, in turn, found myself forced to keep up, to constantly press against the invisible envelope of my own assumed limitations. I didn't have to try and give, they demanded and took. They demanded honesty, respect, knowledge and challenge, and, they had fun while doing it. There was no holding them back. Except—

As the year progressed I would begin to grow concerned about what would happen next year, with another teacher, someone who might not recognize the genius in the child or be able to allow the freedom for growth or expression that was needed. I was concerned about a room full of children that may be unaware of family togetherness, of the cooperation, love and respect that a child from this environment had learned to give and expect in return.

I was concerned and sometimes it would nag at me. I would remind myself that always I must promote awareness and preparation for the "real world" in what we do in our class. They must leave with the skills to help them grow and build upon what they will experience on the other side of the classroom. Of course, part of what the "real world" consists of is what one makes of it in his or her own mind. The world is what you think it is. Thoughts are real things, dreams do come true, and there are no limits. We truly make our own reality.

My dream was that I could be influential in stimulating good thoughts, wonderful dreams and enough self-love in my kids, so that they would allow themselves the strength to always push on those phantasmagorical boundaries and help make this world a little better reality for themselves and those whom they meet.

"You said that all in one breath."

"I know. Pretty good, huh?"

"Remember the time you misspelled intelligence on the board?"

"I misspelled a lot of things on the chalk board—I'm trying to forget about . . . "

"Why? Why forget them, I mean. It was fun."

"You're right. It was fun."

"It was fun. Lots of fun."

Yeah.

Notice

This book is intended to provide information and ideas. The concepts, ideas, techniques, methods or ways of presenting curriculum and/or interacting with students, such as practiced by the author, are not intended as a manual for teaching. The purpose of this book is to educate and entertain.

You are urged to read all available material and learn as much as possible about children and education. This text should be used only as a general guide for developing your own individual teaching style and/or method of relating to children.

Index

AAAs: 45–48
Ants: 26–27
Art: 25–28
Assignment Packet: 25, 52
Babbler: 129
Bank: 15–16, 88–91
Boxes: 83–85
Boycott: 16–18
Buscaglia, Dr. Leo: 22
Chipmunk: 84–85, 99, 101
Classroom sale: 15–18
Class Structure: 124
Communication: 75, 79
Community Work Experience: 50, 69, 76–78
Creep: 97–98
Death: 88–89
Dictionaries: 122
Dock: 15, 36
Donations: 15, 36
Encyclopedia: 23
End of School: 131–132
Epilogue: 134–139
Feast: 70–71
First Day of School: 35, 58, 134–139
Fit: 39–40
Free Time: 62–65, 94–95
Fun: 15–144
Hanging: 99–101
Highrise: 15, 36
Hmm: 57
Hoax: 55–56, 104–107
Home at school: 37
Homework: 58–59
Humor: 114, 15–144
I Believe In You: 96
Insubordination: 75
Interruption: 116
Lamps: 86
Landlords: 15–18
Lie: 54–56
Lucy: 89–92, 111
Marks: 15–16, 67–68, 94
Mechanic's Shop: 17, 36, 112–113, 115–119
Misspelling: 121–122, 139
Mural Painting: 80–82
Music: 19–20
Newspaper Reporter: 108–111
Notice: 140
Nutrition: 66
Open House: 120–122
Picked Last: 102–103
Poetry: 38, 41–44, 133
Preface: 11
Principal: 17–18, 33–34, 37, 80, 107, 119
Private School: 72
Project Box: 64, 67–69
Reading Area: 35–36
Reading Time Warp: 19–21

Science Fair: 105–107
Secretaries: 45, 47, 49–51,
63–64, 69, 88-92
Shoelace Tying: 52–53
Solitude: 65, 72–74
Son: 125–127
Sports: 21, 39–40, 84, 95,
99–101
Standing on Desk: 60–61
Stereo: 19
Store: 15, 93–94
Teachings: 22–24
Think Tank: 128–130
TV Documentary: 121
Video Documentary: 120–121
Visitors: 49–50
Wall Squares: 80–82
Whiz Kids: 122
Write-in Books: 30–34

About The Author

Dr. R. Hawk Starkey is a Behavioral Therapist, Counselor, and Education Consultant with over twenty years experience. He has been a classroom teacher of various grade levels, a school counselor, teacher trainer, and a private practitioner for child and school related problems.

Dr. Starkey is the writer and director of an educational TV film that has been used for teacher training at the university level. The author and his lovely wife live in Austin, Texas, and travel as consultants, speakers and presenters of workshops and seminars on such topics as: More Effective Education for teachers and parents; Health and Nutrition; How State of Mind Can Effect Health; Success Consciousness; and Management Effectiveness Training.

If you would like Dr. Starkey to speak to your group or organization, or would like to order additional books, write to Inreach Publishing, P.O. Box 33280, #288, Austin, Texas, 78764.